Motherland

Motherland

a memoir

LIVING WITH CHILD LOSS AND
BECOMING A MOTHER AGAIN AT 57

Barb Higgins

atmosphere press

Published by Atmosphere Press

Cover design by Kevin Stone

Atmospherepress.com

For all the grieving mothers

A Note from Barb:

This is my account of what happened in the lead up to Molly's death and in the years that followed. These experiences and my interpretation of what happened to Molly are personal and therefore subjective. Although this is the truest account that I can give, I realize that the story I'm telling is my own. At no time in the memoir do I place any blame for Molly's death on the doctors, nurses, or hospitals who cared for her. The purpose of this book is to share my experience of motherhood and grief.

Where necessary and to protect the privacy of those involved in certain parts of this story, I've changed or omitted the names of people and places.

*It seems to me, that if we love, we grieve. That's the deal.
That's the pact. Grief and love are forever intertwined.
Grief is the terrible reminder of the depths of our love and,
like love, grief is non-negotiable.*

– Nick Cave

PART I:

WHAT HAPPENED

A Thousand Tiny Steps

There are two things I've learned from losing my thirteen-year-old daughter, Molly.

The first is that no event takes place in isolation.

When the impossible happens, like our child dying, we act as though it came out of the blue. We say that we were blindsided. That the rug was pulled out from under us. That we didn't see it coming. We act shocked. We're not the people this kind of thing happens to, we say. I'm not the kind of mother who's meant to have a dead child.

Of course, none of this is true.

Nothing ever arrives out of the blue. Not the good things. Or the really bad things. I know that now. I know that everything is more connected than we could ever imagine, that there's an intricate network of threads between each moment, each decision, and every living thing. I know that there are a thousand tiny steps that lead to things that happen to us, to the greatest losses in our lives. And that from every one of those moments, there are another thousand tiny steps to a place of healing—to new life.

It takes a particular kind of attention to see those steps. A kind of aerial view of our lives like the perspective an astronaut has of the earth from space, where everything suddenly makes a kind of sense, even though we can't explain it. That those steps redraw the boundaries between countries, between land and sea. That underneath it all, there's a place that connects every thought and word, every moment to every living thing. I call it Motherland.

The second thing I now know to be true is this: that there's nothing sacred or holy or untouchable about a mother who loses a child.

We deify grieving mothers. Perhaps it all goes back to Mary watching her son dying on the cross: when a mother must face that most cruel and unnatural of tragedies, the death of her child, it somehow turns her into a saint. We look at her suffering and her grief and her survival of this tragedy with admiration. She must be superhuman, we think, to get through this. We even go so far as to think that maybe there's a reason why she was picked to go through this rather than the rest of us mortals with living, breathing children. You're so brave, people say. If it were me, I don't know how I'd survive it. You're incredible for getting through all this.

Grieving mothers are special and holy and sacred: that's the narrative we like to spin.

The reality couldn't be more different.

The grieving mother is as lost and terrified and broken and flawed as the next person. Sometimes more so. Sometimes the grief makes us not more holy but less so. We turn to our baser selves rather than our higher selves. We go to the dark places, often places we went to before the child loss, places that bring immediate comfort and relief. Only this time, the stakes are higher, and so is the fall.

My dark place was addiction.

To drugs. To alcohol. And to the poor choices, often surrounding men, that accompanied those addictions.

I'd do anything to turn back the clock. To re-write the story of the months leading up to Molly's death and those months that followed her death too. I'd do anything to make sure I was the mother she needed and deserved. I wish that I had savored every moment with her. I wish that I'd always been loving and patient and kind. I wish that I'd made her feel seen and understood. I wish that we'd argued less. I wish that when I lay beside her on the hospital bed after the life support machine was turned off, waiting for her heart to stop, I'd been able to feel at peace, knowing that I'd been a good mother. Though, of course, there is no such thing. A good mother is as much of a fabrication as the saintly grieving mother. We are always no more or less than ourselves. Beautiful and broken. Extraordinary and flawed. Less than we would like to be, and at times, more too.

The year leading up to Molly's death was awful. Kenny, my husband, had put us into such debt that I had no choice but to divorce him to secure our family home, my savings, my livelihood. But he wasn't the only one to blame. I was in a relationship with Roy, a man I'd loved and dated, on and off, for six years. Neither Molly nor her fifteen-year-old sister, Gracie, liked him. He was possessive and controlling and kept trying to pull me away from my children. Often, I let him.

Kenny and I took turns to live with Molly and her sister, Gracie, in our family home and in the apartment we'd rented a few miles away. One week Kenny was there, the other week I was. Kenny and I couldn't live under the same roof anymore. I kept telling myself that, any moment now, my life was going to blow up. I felt it in my bones, that something bad was going to happen. But still, I kept making bad decisions.

Kenny drank heavily, even though he was on dialysis, even though his kidneys were failing. If anyone was going to die, I told myself at that time, it was him. He was in late-stage renal failure. I assumed that the gut feeling I had that something bad was going to happen was connected to him. But that's the trouble with those terrible, prescient feelings: they're often realized in ways you could never have imagined. It wasn't Kenny who was about to die.

I also drank too much. And I took recreational drugs. I kept poor company. In the week leading up to Molly's death, in the last days of my thirteen-year-old daughter's life, I was three thousand miles away from her in Europe. I was in another man's bed when Kenny called me to say that our daughter was in the hospital. That I needed to come home immediately.

And in the years after Molly's death, I wasn't any better. I didn't suddenly become wise and good, purified by the tragedy of losing my child. I fell into addiction again. I let people down, most of all Gracie, who deserved better. And of course, I let myself down too.

But at some point, when the madness of grief turned to something else, not a resignation or acceptance—never that—but maybe the ability to lift my head just a little on wobbly legs, I tentatively took a new step. One tiny step forward. A step toward another kind of life. And that step, too, I know, is connected to the thousand tiny steps that came before. I believe that without Molly, there would never have been Jack, the two-year-old sitting at my feet now. Which doesn't make any of it better. It doesn't take the pain away. It doesn't justify Molly's death. It doesn't bring her back, which is what I still wish for every second of every day. But it's a step forward. A tiny step forward in this strange and dark and beautiful and complicated place I called Motherland. A tiny step toward life.

Chapter 1

The Pink Dress

It was low in the back. Sleeveless. Fitted at the top. An empire waist. The pink dress that Molly would be buried in.

When I got back to the house on Sunday morning, Gracie greeted me with a hug. I held her tight and breathed in her skin. I was so glad to be home.

My mom had been staying with Gracie while my ex-husband, Kenny, Molly's dad, drove behind the ambulance to the hospital. He was already in the ER of the local hospital in our town in New Hampshire with Molly.

I grabbed my car keys. "Let's go," I said to Gracie.

I needed to get to Molly. She'd been sick all night, lying on the bathroom floor, throwing up, her headaches so bad she couldn't keep her eyes open, and I hadn't been there for her.

"Before we go, you just have to see the dress, Mom," Gracie said, taking my hand.

Gracie was so excited to show me that I went with it. And I told myself, *Molly's in the hospital now; she's in good hands. A few more minutes away from her won't hurt.*

"Sure," I said, following her up the stairs.

I'd planned out the whole week for the girls while I was in Amsterdam. On the afternoon of Gracie's birthday, they went to the Rockingham Mall with my mom and my sister, Johanna. I'd left them some money, so they could treat themselves.

Molly and Gracie had texted me pictures. I remember thinking that Molly looked haggard, which supported what Kenny said about her headaches. The picture haunts me now. Why didn't I say something? Why hadn't I forced Kenny to bring Molly into the ER earlier? Why hadn't I just flown home?

They'd bought other things that day too. Bath salts and candles and a swan floaty that we'd use in our pool for a few years after Molly died until it got a hole in it.

And the dress.

Gracie and Molly weren't just sisters, they were best friends. Two halves of a whole. Although they were born two years apart, they may well have been twins. Gracie was so excited about the dress, it could have been her own.

"Molly hung it on the back of your bedroom door," Gracie said. "She wanted it to be the first thing you saw when you came home."

Gracie took the dress off the hanger and held it out.

"Isn't it pretty, Mom?" Gracie said.

It was gorgeous. An Audrey Hepburn-style dress. Elegant, like Molly. And pink, her favorite color.

I would wonder later if these things had worked against Molly. Her feminine elegance. Her love of pink. The fact, quite simply, that she was a girl.

"Just wait until you see her in it," Gracie said. Her eyes shone.

I smiled and took Gracie's arm. "Come on, let's go to the hospital."

She nodded and hung the dress back on the door.

I told myself that in a few hours, when the doctors had found out what was wrong with Molly, when they'd given her some medication to make her feel better, we'd all come back home. And once we'd caught up on some sleep, Molly would put on the dress and twirl around the house for us. I'd tell her that I was sorry that I went to Amsterdam and that I was sorry I wasn't there when she needed me last night. She'd give me a hard time about it:

I told you not to go.

But she'd forgive me, and she'd keep twirling around in her beautiful pink dress and we'd move on with our lives.

I looked at Gracie. She was still in her PJs.

"Why don't you get dressed?" I asked.

"It's OK, I'll just throw some shoes on," Gracie said, believing, like me, that we'd be back home soon. That everything was going to turn out OK.

Chapter 2

The First Doctor's Visit

Two months before Molly died—a Sunday too—I'd brought her to see an on-call pediatrician. I'd hoped that Molly's regular physician, whom we loved, was available, but it was a Sunday, and he was at home.

I was at a rowing competition in Boston with Kenny when Molly called to say that she'd been having headaches again.

"Whenever I stand up, my head hurts," she told me on the phone. "I have to grab my head to make it feel better."

Her voice was wobbly. Molly didn't complain, she played down pain and discomfort. So, I knew this was serious.

I jumped in the car and drove home, calling the doctor's office over and over until I finally got through to the on-call physician. After I'd described Molly's symptoms, there was a pause on the line. And then her voice came through:

"I go home at noon," she said.

I wondered whether she'd heard me right.

"Molly's feeling really sick," I said again. "She needs to see a doctor today."

"Sure, but the office closes at twelve."

I checked the clock on the dashboard. I was fifteen minutes away. I had to stop and grab Molly at home, but if we hurried, we'd make it just in time.

I pressed on the accelerator. "We'll be there," I said and hung up.

~

"I'm not one of those mothers who thinks every headache is a brain tumor," I told the doctor that Sunday in February.

I used those words.

I wanted her to know that I wasn't the type of mother to fuss. I was a high school health educator. An athletic coach. I understood teenagers. I knew the difference between a kid who was faking it and a kid who was in pain.

And I wanted her to know that this was more than Molly just having a headache. That if Molly had asked me to drive the hour and a half back from Boston to the town in central New Hampshire where we lived, something must be wrong.

The physician turned to Molly.

"Are you the kind of girl who complains a lot about things?" she asked her.

Molly's eyes widened.

"No ..." she started, "I ... I don't think so ..."

She kept going:

"Do you like to tell your mother about every little thing that's wrong?"

"What? No. You're not listening—" I interrupted.

The doctor ignored me and kept looking at Molly.

Molly had a big medical file. In February 2015, she'd been diagnosed with Bell's palsy. It turned out that she probably had Lyme disease: the two are often connected in children. One half of her face sagged a little. She was self-conscious about it; like every teenage girl, Molly liked to look pretty. She was worried people would notice in her dance shows. At night, we had to tape shut one of her eyes, so she could sleep. I wonder, now, whether it was all somehow connected to the brain tumor.

A few months after that, Gracie and Molly had their annual physicals with their pediatrician, whom they loved. There's an anxiety scale they use for teenagers: Molly scored high. I wasn't surprised. Molly worried about things. Like homework. Like kids at school not being treated fairly. She was sensitive. She wanted to get things right and got upset when she didn't. And she was an empathetic kid. Whenever anyone was unhappy, she felt it and tried to do something about it. Anyway, I guess our doctor had put that in her file too: that she was an anxious kid.

Molly told her about how the headaches had made her throw up.

Molly was skinny by nature. And on top of that, she'd lost more weight recently.

Molly scored on the top end of the anxiety chart.

Later, we found out that the doctor's conclusion was that Molly had an eating disorder. It was perhaps an obvious diagnosis for a skinny, anxious teenage girl, but it turned out that Molly's symptoms—headaches, weight loss—were all also classic symptoms of a brain tumor.

"I think we should x-ray her head," I suggested. "Just to rule things out. Something's not right."

The doctor turned back to me. She raised her eyebrows.

"We don't typically do scans on a first visit."

I shrank back. I'd obviously said the wrong thing.

She glanced up at the clock. I felt I could read her thoughts. She should have been home already. It was a Sunday. She wanted to be with her family. We were intruding on her personal time. I understood, I valued my Sundays too. But I was so worried about Molly.

"Bring her in again in two or three weeks if the symptoms persist or get worse."

Molly was quiet on the drive home. I felt that she was still in pain, but it was more than that too.

I reached out and squeezed her hand.

"I'm sorry, Molly, that really didn't help, did it?" I said.

She bowed her head and looked into her lap.

"It's OK, Mom," she said. "At least you believed me."

~

There would be two more doctor's visits before Molly was admitted to the ER. Kenny brought her to both.

The first took place three days before I left for Amsterdam.

It was early in the morning. I went into the girls' room to wake Molly. She leaped up off the bed and ran to the bathroom and threw up in the toilet. For the next two hours, she threw up repeatedly. Every twenty minutes or so, she'd rush to the bathroom, her vomiting so violent that she often missed the toilet bowl. She said her tongue was numb. She said that her vision was blurred. There were squiggly lines behind her eyelids. And that her head hurt so, so much.

The earliest doctor's appointment we could get was at 2:00 that afternoon. I was teaching, so Kenny took Molly.

Again, Molly's regular pediatrician wasn't available.

When Kenny and Molly came home from that second visit, I could see that Molly was upset.

"The doctor told me that I was too skinny. That I should eat more. That I was dehydrated."

On the way home, Kenny and Molly had stopped by the grocery store to buy some nuts and some Gatorade.

"She said I was anorexic," Molly said, sobbing. "I'm not anorexic."

I held her in my arms and stroked her head. "I know, I know."

For the next few weeks, Molly did what she was told. She ate the nuts. She drank the Gatorade. She put on a little weight. For long periods of time, the headaches didn't come back, and we thought she was OK, that it had passed, that maybe the headaches were a developmental phase.

But they came back again, out of nowhere, the pain knocking her off her feet.

~

The pain came back, worse than ever before, when I was in Amsterdam on what was meant to be a romantic week away with Roy. He was always urging me to go away with him, to leave the girls. He liked to have me to himself. He'd booked the tickets as a surprise. I'd tried to talk him out of it. To talk myself out of it. I knew it was wrong to go, even though I didn't yet know why. But Roy was persuasive. He loved me. He wanted time with me. He'd paid for it all already. And so, two days before I was due to return, Molly ran to the bathroom and vomited from the pain in her head.

Again, Kenny took her to the pediatrician. Again, ours wasn't available. Again, Molly was sent home and we were told that she was fine, that she just had migraines.

That night I called Kenny from Amsterdam to get an update.

"The doctor gave Molly a pamphlet on meditation," Kenny said. Then there was a pause. "Molly threw it out of the window on the drive home."

Molly was angry. Three times now she'd gone to the doctor to say that she was in pain. That the headaches were unbearable. That the vomiting, when the headaches came on so suddenly, was unbearable. That there were times when she couldn't stand up without needing to hold her head. That she felt dizzy. That her tongue tingled with numbness. The pain was unbearable.

Chapter 3
Stop Asking

When Gracie and I got to the ER on that Sunday morning in May, I ran straight over to Molly. I hugged her and kissed her and whispered in her ear:

"I'm here, Molly. I'm here now."

Her eyes were closed. She had one hand over her brow, but she raised the other arm straight up to let me know she'd heard. For now, Molly was conscious enough to communicate with me. That would change rapidly in the next few hours.

"I love you, Mama," she said.

"I love you too, Molly Dolly."

I remembered our last exchange a week ago, before I left for Amsterdam. She was mad at me for going off with Roy. At the fact that he was taking me away from her. And she was angry that I would be missing Gracie's birthday. She didn't spell it out, but I knew what she was trying to say: I was choosing him over them.

In the hours before I left for Amsterdam, Gracie and I snuggled on my bed. I said I was sorry. That Roy hadn't known when he'd booked the trip that it would coincide with her birthday. I promised that we'd celebrate when I got back. Molly refused to join in.

"You can't keep me here by doing this," I told her. "But if something happens to me while I'm away, you'll be sad that we didn't say goodbye."

It was our family rule: no matter how angry we got at each other, we never walked out without saying "I love you."

Molly turned to me and said, "I hope you have a good time, Mom, but I need you to know that I'm disappointed in your choices."

~

Molly was wiser than the rest of us put together. Maybe she even knew on some level that nothing would happen to me. That if someone was going to get hurt in all this, it would be her.

An ER nurse was administering meds prescribed by the first doctor we saw that day, the female ER doctor Kenny spoke to when he first brought Molly in.

"This will make you feel better, Molly," the nurse told her.

"We've given her a mix of Compazine, Benadryl, and Toradol for her migraine," the nurse explained to us. "She'll feel better soon."

A bad migraine. That's what they thought she had.

As I listened to the ER doctor, I told myself to calm down. She was the expert. She knew how to diagnose a patient. It was her job to care for Molly. It drowned out all the other voices in my head telling me that Molly wasn't OK and that they should be doing more for her. That this latest episode she'd had—vomiting non-stop on the bathroom floor between 3:30 a.m. and 6:30 a.m.—it was different. It was worse than a migraine.

This conditioning we have to trust our doctors, it goes deep. As does our belief that they are the experts when it comes to our bodies and the bodies of our children. Greater experts, we tell ourselves than we are, their mothers, the mothers who conceived them and carried them for nine months and birthed them and raised them for thirteen years. The white coat and the medical degree supersede a mother's knowledge and a mother's intuition. Perhaps, because of my own insecurities, that was the message I was receiving. And I believed it. Sometimes I still believe it. I have a deep admiration for the medical profession, for those who care for us when we are sick. I so wanted them to make Molly better.

In the ER, I sat down next to Molly, took her hand, and held it to my face and prayed that all this would be over soon.

The hours blurred into each other.

Gracie, Kenny, and I waited while Molly slept.

I was on a health kick, doing 100 burpees a day, so I did a few on the floor of Molly's room. Gracie took some selfies with Molly.

"I'll embarrass her with these when she wakes up," Gracie joked, smiling at her phone.

We acted as though everything was going to turn out fine. That later that day, we'd be walking out of the ER with Molly and that our lives would go back to normal.

Every now and then, a nurse would come in to check on Molly.

"Do you feel better?" One of them asked her.

"No," she said, her voice feeble.

"On a scale of one to ten, how bad is the pain?"

"Ten," she said, her voice so quiet we could barely make out her answer.

Surely the pain meds should have some effect, I thought? And surely, if she was in this much pain, they should be doing more to help her?

Then the nurse leaned over the bed and said, "Open your eyes, Molly. Wiggle your toes. Grip my fingers."

Feebly, Molly obeyed.

"Is it normal that she's this sleepy?" I asked.

"It's the migraine medication," the nurse replied. "It'll wear off."

With every hour that passed, with every nurse or doctor who came in and checked on Molly, I watched her get less responsive. The meds were meant to be wearing off; she was meant to be waking up, but instead, she was sinking deeper into herself.

~

That afternoon, I drove back to the house with Gracie while Kenny stayed with Molly. Gracie got changed and then decided to stay home to do some homework. She still believed that she'd be going back to school on Monday. I went back to the ER, swapped places with Kenny, and had some time alone with Molly.

I sat next to her, holding her hand, talking to her, telling her I loved her, waiting and hoping that she'd wake up.

Instead, she grew sleepier.

After what seemed like hours, another doctor came by, a pediatric hospitalist working a twenty-four-hour shift. He told us that he'd been consulting with the ER doctor, that he was up to speed on Molly's case.

I sat up. "Oh, thank goodness, I've been waiting for you to come. Molly's really not right."

And then I asked the question I asked over and over during those sixteen hours when Molly was in the ER. The one that I'd asked two months ago, that Sunday in February, sitting with Molly in the pediatrician's office.

"I think we should do a CT scan," I said. "I'm convinced there's something wrong with her brain."

I wasn't a doctor. But I knew. I just knew.

He shook his head. "We don't do CT scans on children. There's too much radiation."

"Well, an MRI then. She needs to be checked out; she's barely conscious."

"The meds are making her sleepy, that's all," he said.

"But I thought the meds were meant to be wearing off?" I swallowed hard. "Please. I want her to have a scan."

He looked at me and said, "There are no neurological grounds for a scan. We need to wait for the meds to wear off, then we can do a proper assessment."

~

As I had so many times already and as I would in the following hours and days, I questioned myself. Was I overreacting? Was I asking for something unreasonable? Were my feelings about my daughter's condition somehow wrong?

I watched him leave the room and go on with his rounds and sat back down next to Molly.

~

Over the next few hours, as Molly's condition got worse, nurses and doctors came in and out of her room and nothing changed. They just kept playing the same record, repeatedly:

We need to wait.

The meds are making her sleepy.

There's no need for a scan.

One of the nurses looked me in the eye and said, "She's stable. She's safe. Stop asking."

~

I so wanted to believe him.

At 6:00 p.m., a new doctor came on shift. I watched her read Molly's notes. The migraines and the medication. The pregnancy and the drugs tests, both of which were negative. Molly had never even kissed a boy. She was scared of smoking and alcohol, would never go near drugs. The suspected eating disorder.

Of course, she looked emaciated: she'd been throwing up on a bathroom floor all night. And she'd been struggling so hard with her headaches, they'd made her feel so sick that she'd lost her appetite.

~

By 6:30 p.m., Molly was spiking a fever.

I still had the words of the male nurse ringing in my ears: *She's stable. She's safe. Stop asking.*

But I couldn't stop. I felt that Molly was getting worse.

"Please," I begged, "something's not right. I really think Molly should have an MRI now."

It was a deep, invisible, tugging feeling that had grown through the day. I remembered the A.A. Milne poems I'd learned by heart as a child. I identified with the way the characters expressed their anxiety. Eeyore was glum, and that wasn't me; I'm an optimist by nature. But I understood the fears that Pooh and Piglet expressed. And the foreboding. *Tut, tut, it looks like rain.* They knew. *I* knew. Something wasn't right. And something bad, something I couldn't stop, was coming.

The doctor looked up from her notes. "We've scheduled an outpatient MRI for Monday."

"But why can't you do an MRI now?"

She glanced at the clock. "The MRI machine is only available until 4:00 p.m. on Sundays."

"But this is the ER—" I started. "Surely nothing should ever be closed in the ER."

"Molly's stats are fine," she said. "She's responding. The best thing we can do is to wait and see how she does once the meds have worn off."

And then she put away her notes and left.

I looked over at Molly. Every hour, more color drained from her face. And her body had become so still.

That voice in my head, the mother's voice, the one that the doctors and nurses had been trying to drown out for hours now, it was getting louder. If Molly didn't start getting better soon, I'd break down the door to the MRI and do the scan myself.

Chapter 4

Someone on Our Side

Kenny and Gracie came back to be with me and Molly. And still, we waited. The meds should have worn off by now, I kept thinking. Molly should have been waking up.

At times, it felt like we'd been forgotten. A request had been put in for Molly to be moved up to the pediatric ward and since then, no ER staff had been in to see us.

Finally, at 11:00 p.m., Molly was given a room in pediatrics. She'd been in the ER for fourteen hours.

Relief flooded my body. At least here, she'd get specialist care.

A pediatric nurse, whom I will call Angel, came in. She went straight over to Molly.

"Open your eyes, Molly," she said.

Her tone was kind and gentle. I felt my body relaxing for the first time since I entered the hospital.

"Molly, can you try to open your eyes for me?" she repeated.

Molly's eyes flickered open for a second and then closed again.

Angel moved down to the side of the bed.

"Grip my fingers," she said, placing her fingers in Molly's palm.

Molly's fingers curled up lightly. She was trying.

Angel walked to the foot of the bed.

"Wiggle your toes."

Molly's feet didn't move.

"Wiggle your toes for me now, Molly."

Still nothing.

I began to panic. Molly should be responding to all three neurological tests.

"Can you move your toes for me, Molly?" she asked again.

I willed for her to move, but her legs lay still in the bedsheets.

I glanced over at Gracie and Kenny. They looked lost in their thoughts; they weren't on high alert like I was.

"I don't like what I'm seeing," Angel said. "She should be more responsive."

At last, I thought, my breath settling for the first time since we got to the ER.

At last, someone's looking at Molly with the same eyes that I am, as a mother. It was comforting to me to see someone paying so much attention to Molly.

I jumped up.

"That's what I've been saying—" I started. "There's something wrong. I know there is. It's not just the meds."

And that's when Molly's limbs began thrashing. My heart leaped to my throat. *She's waking up*, I thought.

Gracie jumped up from her chair.

"Look, Mom!" she said. "She's moving!"

We took a video of her to show her later. They looked kind of funny, those involuntary jerky movements. We thought it would make Molly laugh.

That's how convinced we were that she was going to be fine: we took a video to show her when she woke up. We look through those photos and videos from the ER now and they haunt us. We really believed she would be OK.

Kenny came up to the bed too. I could tell he was relieved that Molly was waking up. It was time for all this to be over and for us to go back home.

Then the thrashing stopped.

And Molly went very still.

I looked over at Angel. I could tell from the expression in her eyes that she hadn't interpreted Molly's thrashing in the way we had. She didn't look excited about Molly waking up, she looked worried.

A myoclonic seizure, that's the medical term for what happened to Molly's body in those few seconds when we thought she was coming back to us. But that wasn't an indication that she was getting better; it was a sign that her nervous system was shutting down. But I didn't know that then. I was still happy that she'd moved. I thought I was going to get my Molly back.

I turned to Gracie and Kenny. "Why don't you go home and get some sleep? I'll call you if anything happens."

I believed that we were in the home stretch. That this was the first step in Molly getting better. That Gracie and Kenny didn't need to stay here, holding vigil at Molly's bedside because soon she'd be coming home to us. We agreed that Gracie should probably stay home from school tomorrow because she'd be tired and because Molly would need time to recuperate too. But she needed to eat something and to rest. They'd go to the grocery store in the morning. Kenny would cook them some dinner.

After Gracie and Kenny left, Angel turned to me and said, "I'll get the hospitalist. I'd like him to re-examine Molly."

"OK," I said.

I was still hopeful—then. Molly had shown signs of waking up, hadn't she? And the doctors could finally work out what was wrong with her and make her better.

Chapter 5

It's Too Late

It was 1:30 on Monday morning when Angel came back with the hospitalist. They were very quiet.

I'd noticed some blood around Molly's nostrils, so I mentioned it.

"Molly gets nosebleeds all the time," I said.

It was one of the few symptoms Molly had that day that I wasn't worried about. She was a kid who got nosebleeds. This didn't seem out of the ordinary for Molly. Later, I found out that it was brain-stem pressure that had caused the blood.

Angel repeated her threefold inspection.

"Open your eyes for me, Molly. Grip my fingers. Wiggle your toes."

This time, there was nothing.

"I don't like what I'm seeing, Molly," she said.

The hospitalist pulled Angel over to one side and started whispering. I listened in. I wasn't going to be pushed out of any conversation about Molly.

"We need to prep her for a scan," he said.

I couldn't believe what I was hearing.

I leapt out of my chair.

"*What*?"

He turned to me and said, "We're going to prep Molly for a CT scan."

"You're going to give her a scan? Why *now*? I've been asking you to do that ever since she got here." I glanced at the clock. "I've been asking for sixteen hours!"

"Molly's vitals have changed," he said. "We need to do a scan."

"I was told that CT scans involved too great a risk of radiation for kids."

He stared at me. "Molly's symptoms are presenting differently now. We need to do the scan."

This is what I read between the lines: when weighed with the seriousness of her condition, radiation damage was worth the risk. It told me everything I needed to know about the seriousness of her condition.

I was scared. They kept saying that she had a migraine. That she didn't need a scan. And now they were walking around with panic written all over their faces.

And alongside the fear, I was angry. Why couldn't they have just listened to me to begin with?

Angel inserted a catheter in Molly. I took her hand and, as I watched the fluid leaving her body and filling the bowl, I looked down at Molly's legs. The hairs on the back of my neck flew up. A few minutes before, she'd been thrashing around. Now, there was no movement at all. *Her legs are so still*, I remember thinking. Like they'd melted into the bedsheets.

I turned my head toward Molly's head and that's when I noticed that the color of her skin had changed.

"Why's she so yellow?" I asked.

They didn't answer.

"Why's Molly yellow?" I said, louder.

I kept staring at her face. It wasn't yellow now, it was gray. And her lips were turning a dark brown. Then purple. Then navy blue.

My body started shaking.

"Her face, there's no color in her face. Her lips!" I yelled.

A machine behind Molly started making a noise.

A nurse pushed me out of the way and pressed a button. I could tell that she was freaking out. We both were. The button set off an alarm that signaled to her team that there was a code blue. Although I did not know it at the time, Molly was going into cardiac arrest.

The room flooded with doctors and nurses. They jostled me out of the way.

"You need to get out," one of the nurses said to me.

"I'm staying," I said.

I watched them get out the paddles. I watched them tear off Molly's clothes. I looked at her skinny, naked body. Her small breasts. I thought again about how modest she was. How much she'd be embarrassed, how she'd hate for her privacy to be violated like this.

They shocked her heart over and over.

I got on the phone with Kenny. He and Gracie had just started drifting off to sleep.

"Something's wrong with Molly!" My voice shook. "She's not breathing!"

"We're coming back," Kenny said. "I'll get Gracie."

And then I hung up.

The doctors and nurses were standing over Molly, holding their breath, the paddles raised above Molly's chest, ready to shock her again. And then the lines on the heart monitor went jagged.

"She's back," one of the nurses said.

The room breathed out.

Her heart was beating again. They intubated her to help her breathe.

In films, when you see doctors jump-starting someone's heart, you're made to believe that they've raised a patient from the dead, that they've used their human tools to play God. In our world, doctors are gods.

I know now that a heart can keep beating in a dead body. That the lines between life and death are blurred. And that what really matters in the end is what's happening in the patient's brain.

I also know now that doctors aren't gods. Not even close. They're as human as the rest of us.

While the hospitalist and Angel were preparing Molly for the CT scan that she should have had sixteen hours ago, the buildup of fluid had put so much pressure on her brain stem that the tumor had ruptured. The tumor that no one yet knew was there.

~

It was 3:00 a.m. when the hospital called a neurological specialist from another town. Later, he told us that if he'd received that call about an adult, he wouldn't have bothered coming in: the prognosis was too bad. But Molly was thirteen. You go the extra mile for children.

He took Molly away to drain the fluid from her brain and then he came back and called us to one of the many meetings we'd have with doctors and nurses over the coming days. The delivery-of-bad news meetings. My mother had arrived with a friend whom we asked to stay with Gracie while the neurologist spoke to us.

We followed him to the family room, and that's where he said the words that still don't make sense to me now, six years after Molly's death:

"I'm sorry. We're too late."

My brain started spinning. A few hours ago, they told us that Molly had a migraine. That I should stop fussing. That I was being too pushy, asking for a brain scan. And now they were telling me that it was *too late?*

Maybe I wasn't understanding this right.

"Too late for what?" I asked.

"The buildup of fluid caused such a large rupture in Molly's brain. The damage is extensive. We don't believe she's going to wake up."

I tried to step out of myself. It's what I'd always done when something bad happened. When I was a little girl, scared by the relative who came into my room at night when my mother was away. When I ran professionally, and the physical pain got too much to bear. When I couldn't stand being me, being Barb. I had to find some way to distance myself from the words that this next doctor had just told me. That Molly had died.

Only it didn't work. I would find ways later to cope with this kind of living, to exist in the world with the knowledge that Molly was dead. But right now, I stayed inside myself and I didn't know how I could survive it.

I climbed onto the table and crawled toward the doctor until my face was right up close to his. I heard a noise, someone screaming, a noise I had never heard before. It was me. I was screaming *No! No! No!*

Maybe if I yelled loud enough. Maybe if he saw how crazy I was. Maybe if I showed him what it meant to lose Molly, I could turn back time and make it all OK again.

The doctor didn't react. See it often enough and human trauma becomes routine.

No! No! No! I kept yelling, shaking my head.

I wanted him to change his mind. To say that he'd got it wrong. That he was going to try something else. That he'd made a mistake, he'd been working on the wrong patient. It wasn't Molly who'd died.

When he still said nothing, I crawled down off the table, crawled across the floor, and along the wall. I peed myself. I told myself over and over that it couldn't be too late, that there had to be something they could do to save Molly.

I heard one of the nurses telling my mother that she'd get me some medication. A Xanax. Something to calm me down.

"No," my mother said. "Leave her be."

Mom had been a nurse. She knew that no one should medicate me out of this pain. Later, there'd be a time to numb myself to the truth of what happened. But right now, I needed to feel it.

The neurologist started talking again.

"I've organized a transfer for Molly to a specialist at a children's hospital an hour north."

This didn't make sense to me.

"What? But you just said it was too late."

"Yes. I believe it is. But we should remove the tumor. It's unlikely, but it might have some impact on her brain activity."

I straightened up.

"So, there's a chance she might be OK?"

"If she were an adult, we wouldn't be doing the transfer."

"But you think this could work?"

"Molly's thirteen. Young bodies are more resilient than ours. We need to give her that chance."

So, there was hope. It wasn't too late after all. She could still wake up and be OK. For the next five days, every cell of my body would cling to that hope. In some ways, even now, six years after Molly's death, I still hope. I still think I'll wake up and that a doctor will walk into my room and say that Molly woke up. That she was fine. That she'll be coming home with us. That her living body will get to wear that pink dress.

Chapter 6

The Three of Us

Even today, seven years later, I still don't know whether we've made any progress in reframing our family, of learning to move through our days without Molly alongside us. But I know that the process began on the drive north in the early hours of that Monday morning.

Molly was meant to be airlifted to the children's hospital, but it started raining, so they had to take her by ambulance instead. It seemed like another obstacle to Molly getting the treatment she deserved. I wanted to go with her in the ambulance, but they wouldn't let me do that either. Perhaps it was to protect me—or to give me a break from sitting next to my unconscious child, thinking about how unlikely it was that she was going to wake up. I gave in, knowing that Gracie needed me.

Gracie, Kenny, and I went home to grab some clothes and to wash and then drove to the children's hospital. Gracie sat beside me up front; Kenny sat in the back.

After breaking down in that family room, I pulled myself together. I was in mom mode again, steering my family through this crisis. I wanted Gracie to be prepared for what lay ahead. As I stared at the rain through the windshield, I walked her through what might happen.

"There are three possible outcomes, Gracie. And we need

to be prepared for any one of them."

She nodded, wordless.

The seriousness of Molly's condition hadn't registered with her yet. A few hours ago, we were talking about Molly going home and trying on her pink dress. A few days before, she'd celebrated her fifteenth birthday with Molly as they danced to Taylor Swift's "Fifteen" around their shared bedroom. I'd think about those lyrics later, about this special time when everything is still open, before you know who you're going to be in the world, how they would ring truer for Gracie than she'd ever imagined.

We still hadn't told Gracie how serious Molly's condition was. She wasn't ready to hear that her sister was dead. None of us were.

"Are you listening to me, Gracie?" I asked.

She nodded again.

"First, Molly could wake up and everything will be OK."

I think that's what Kenny, Gracie, and I still believed would happen. Regardless of everything we'd been through in the last sixteen hours, regardless of the seizure and the rupturing of the brain tumor and her unconsciousness and that neurologist's words, we still believed Molly would come back to us as the same old Molly we knew and loved. We couldn't allow ourselves to believe anything else.

But I still said the other options out loud. Because it was my job as a mom to prepare Gracie. To prepare all of us. And maybe it was my way of forcing myself to face those possibilities too.

"Second," I said, "Molly will wake up, but she'll be a very different Molly from the one we know. She might not be able to use her legs. She might be dizzy all the time. There are things she might not be able to do for herself anymore. There's been a lot of damage to her brain, Gracie. Although I'd love her to come back to us and be just fine, this is probably the most likely outcome. We must be prepared for it."

I felt Gracie sinking into herself.

There was no way we could conceive of Molly being any different from the Molly we'd known a few hours ago. Smart, funny, kind, stubborn, talented Molly. Molly singing and tap dancing and owning the stage. Molly giving me a hard time for not being a good enough mom while at the same time deferring to me for all the important decisions because she knew that, flawed as I was, I put her first and I knew what she needed to be happy. Molly, whose ambition it was to graduate as the valedictorian of her class one day. Molly who got excited by Taylor Swift and scented candles and bubble baths and selfies and a beautiful pink dress and the long summer ahead with the pool in the yard and her friends and the beginning of eighth grade.

But if we had to, we'd take Molly any way she came back to us. As long as we had her, we'd love her, and we'd find the amazing in her even if she couldn't do the things she did before, even if we barely recognized her. Molly was our family. Without her, we didn't make sense.

I took a breath.

"And third, Molly might never wake up."

I could hear the rain falling hard against the car windows. The silence as this third option sat between us.

"We just need to think through what these three scenarios might look like for us as a family," I said. "We need to be ready."

Except there was no being ready. There was only putting one foot in front of the other and surviving. But we didn't know that then, the three of us, a new family, following the ambulance carrying our dear Molly through the dark Monday morning.

Chapter 7

Hope

We arrived at the children's hospital early on Monday morning and went straight to the Pediatric Intensive Care Unit where we were led to Molly's room. She was brought in shortly afterward, her head all bandaged up, her body hooked to a million different machines. I think I knew, looking at her then, and reading the body language of the doctors and nurses, that the neurologist had been right when he said it was too late, that Molly would never wake up.

But at the same time, every cell in my body longed for her to open her eyes.

For the next thirty-six hours, my mind and my heart kept leaping from one state to the other: this deep-seated knowledge that Molly had already died at 1:30 a.m. in our local hospital alongside a desperate clinging to the hope that she would be the miracle. That she would defy the odds. That my amazing Molly would come through and stun us all.

Perhaps everyone thinks they're special. Perhaps that's part of the human condition. Perhaps it's how we survive. We're the heroes of our own stories, and the heroes always make it in the end, don't they?

If there was a thirteen-year-old girl with a ruptured brain tumor who everyone thought was going to die who miraculously made it and went on to dance and act and study and live a full and beautiful life, a girl who'd tell the tale to anyone willing to listen of how she'd overcome the odds, well, of course, it would be Molly. Our sweet, talented, extraordinary Molly. She deserved to survive this.

I knew the truth. I knew she wasn't coming back.

But also, I hoped.

There are times when it's possible-when it's necessary–to live in those contradictory states.

At 9:00 a.m., they took Molly away for the operation to remove her tumor.

She was in surgery for six hours.

While she was away, our friends and family arrived. The news had started to get out about Molly being sick. No one believed that she wasn't going to wake up. They brought food and balloons and flowers. They decorated Molly's room. Gracie welcomed her friends, giddy at the attention. She was the only one of us who hadn't been part of all the meetings at the other hospital; apart from the conversation we'd had with her in the car on the way to the children's hospital, she didn't know how serious Molly's condition was. Looking back, I'm glad we didn't tell her everything right away, that she had these hours to be with her friends and to keep believing that Molly would come back.

At 2:30 p.m., they brought Molly back in. She looked the same. Maybe a little paler. Her body so still.

All afternoon and evening we allowed visitors to come in, two at a time.

Dr. Brooks, who operated on Molly, came to speak to me and Kenny. I was surprised by how hopeful he seemed. Molly didn't need any additional oxygen, he said. Her body was responding well.

"The tumor came out easily," he explained. "And her brain matter looks healthy, it's pink and moist," he said. "It's a good sign."

My heart flickered. For the first time since meeting with

the neurologist in the early hours of the morning, I allowed real hope to set in. Here was a doctor, a specialist, telling me that Molly's brain looked healthy, that the operation had gone well.

"So, what now?" I asked.

"We wait to see some movement. If Molly's brain is healthy, she should slowly be waking up again. It might take some time, but we'll be watching for signs."

"OK," I said.

I'll watch her like a hawk, I remember thinking. I'll be the first to notice a flutter in her eyelids or a twitch in her fingers.

That night, as our first wave of visitors drove back home, we settled in for the night. Gracie and Kenny went to stay in David's House, a place the hospital set up for families who needed to be close to their sick children. I stayed and slept in Molly's room with my friend, Robyn. The nurses had set up a bed for me.

Although I was exhausted, I didn't sleep well. Every hour or so, I'd wake up and check on Molly. I'd look to see if she'd moved. Nurses would come in and do the same.

There's still time, I told myself. She's been through a big operation. A lot of trauma. A ton of meds. We need to give her time.

But there wasn't any response. Not that afternoon or evening after her operation. And not through the night. Molly just lay there, her thin, pale body, stiller than I'd ever seen it.

Chapter 8

Molly's My Patient

At some point that night, when I couldn't sleep, I noticed some boxes of uneaten pizzas in the room. Someone had ordered food for everyone earlier in the day.

I placed the boxes on the counter.

"Hi, I have some extra pizza," I called out.

A male nurse looked up at me from his paperwork. He smiled. "Thanks," he said.

There was something in the way he looked at me that caught my attention.

He came out from behind the nurse's station. He was wearing blue scrubs and running shoes. His movements were so familiar. *I've seen those movements before,* I thought to myself.

I've thought a lot about the nature of memory since Molly died. Especially about how we remember those we love. So much of it lies in the relationship we have to their bodies. To their smell. The texture of their hair. The marks on their skin. How they move through the world. It never leaves us.

I checked the nurse's running shoes. Running had got me a scholarship to BU and, after college, I had run for Nike. For a long time, it was the most important thing in my life.

We were face to face now. I was looking him right in the eye. And then it clicked.

I dropped the bag I was carrying. I threw my arms around him.

"Chaz! How could I not have recognized you?"

He held me tight.

"I wouldn't have recognized you either, Barb. It's been over twenty years. We've both changed. But I read Molly's file, I worked out who you were." He paused. "Molly's my patient."

Molly's my patient.

Using the word luck in the context of Molly's death seems wrong. There is nothing lucky about your child dying. In fact, just about everything about Molly getting sick and ending up in the ER and being taken to the children's hospital had been horrible and ugly. But things were starting to change. In this week, at this hospital, there were things that happened—people that happened— that I now see as miracles. Part of the thousand tiny steps that connect every part of this story. That made this story start long before Molly got sick. Long before she was even born.

That long Monday night, between Molly's operation and everything that would happen on Tuesday, the universe or whatever it is that sometimes looks out for us gave me Chaz.

I hadn't seen him in over twenty years. We'd met after college, when I moved back to New Hampshire. And here he was, on this of all nights.

We'd dated for two and a half years. We'd loved each other. We'd been good to each other. And now he was standing in front of me, a nurse in a PICU miles from where I lived, assigned to take care of Molly.

Back when we were dating, Chaz was a mountain man—he worked for the Appalachian Club. I had no idea that he had trained to become a nurse. After we split up, he met someone else and had a son and now he had a daughter as well, eleven, just two years younger than Molly.

And he wasn't called Chaz anymore. The nurses all referred to him as Charlie. They found it funny, my nickname for him, born all those years ago when we were so close. I guess he'd grown up; we both had.

I believe that the universe is always working out its strange ways with us. Most of the time, we don't notice it. That's probably a good thing. But when life is heightened—when you're in the intensive care unit with your dying daughter—things happen that lift the curtain and allow you to see those workings. Of all the nurses in all of America on all the days of the year, this one, the man I'd loved deeply for years, was Molly's nurse. In the days to come, especially toward the end of our stay at the hospital, Chaz's presence and his actions would save me from my darkest moments. Chaz was one of those thousand tiny steps that carried me through my loss.

Chaz was a gift that night and for the rest of the week too. He'd be with us when we unplugged her. And he'd be the last person with Molly when she was taken away to the morgue on Saturday afternoon. He came in on his day off for me. For Molly.

I will forever feel grateful—and lucky—for that. For him.

Chapter 9

She's Never Going to Dance Again

Early on Tuesday morning, before Molly's friends and our family showed up again, Dr. Brooks, the doctor who'd operated on Molly, came into the room. His body language was a world away from the man who held a meeting with us after Molly's operation. He was slow and guarded, his shoulders stooped.

As he checked on Molly, he didn't say anything. I could tell, from the hushed words he exchanged with the nurse, that they weren't happy with what they were seeing. Molly hadn't moved. That was what they saw.

"If Molly was going to move, she would have done so already," he said.

I felt my guts twist. Not again, I thought. I can't go through this again.

"But you said her brain looked good, you said the operation went well—"

"Yes. But the key is how Molly responds after the operation. If her brain is healthy, she should be moving."

I wanted him to wait. I wanted us to keep hoping. Maybe Molly needed more time to respond to the operation. But I'd watched her all night, I'd seen how still she was.

He sat down on the edge of the bed. He looked me in the

eye and when he spoke, his voice was quiet but stern.

"Why didn't you bring her into the ER earlier?" he asked.

I felt like I'd been punched in the stomach. "What?"

"We only got the call at 1:00 a.m. It took her hours to get here. Why did you wait so long to bring Molly into the ER?"

I took a breath to steady myself.

"We didn't wait to bring her to the ER. We took her to the ER at 9:00 on Sunday morning. We asked for a CT scan," I explained. "They said that she was safe and stable. They told us to wait. To stop asking."

A beat of silence. Doctors, surgeons like Dr. Brooks, watch people die—watch children die—every day. But in his silence, I could feel the enormity of his shock and sadness. This case was different.

Dr. Brooks had tried to fix Molly. He'd operated on her for six hours. He'd hoped that maybe he'd been able to bring her back to life with his skills as a surgeon. But it was too late. There was nothing more he could do. Her brain had died before she arrived here.

In the months that followed, like any mother who loses a child, I'd relive this moment over and over, wondering whether maybe Molly could have been saved, that maybe her death wasn't inevitable.

But at that moment, I wasn't ready to accept that she was dead. That this was the end of the road. Some days, even now, years later, I wake up believing that it's all been a mistake. That Molly's going to be OK. That she'll come running up the driveway and up onto the porch, her backpack swinging off her skinny shoulders, calling for Gracie and bubbling over with news about her day.

That's how grief plays with the mind; it never quite lets us believe that the person we've loved is gone.

The doctor stood up and spoke to the nurse. "Let's prepare Molly for an MRI."

He explained that they needed to see what had happened

up, and told us that she had to speak to her friends. That they needed to know what was going on.

We watched her walk out of the room over to her friends and heard her announce, "Molly's never going to dance again."

~

She tried to explain it to them. Some of her friends didn't understand her words. Maybe Molly had woken up, but there was something wrong with her legs. The mothers were confused.

When I came out of the meeting room, I found her sitting in a circle on the floor, cross-legged with those six Tuesday night girls. They were all holding hands. She was talking them through everything. She'd watched me go into what our friends and family called *Barb Mode* and she was doing the same.

Molly and Gracie took their cues from me. When I was angry, they were angry. When I was sad, they cried too. When I took charge of a situation, they watched and learned. It breaks my heart now, thinking back to how much they trusted me to keep them safe. To do the right thing.

"We're in a state of trauma," Gracie said to her friends. "We need to drink lots of water. Your moms and dads love you most; even though you might not like what they say, you need to listen to them. They're the ones who are here to look after you."

The girls' parents took me aside.

"What's going on?" they said. "No one's told us anything."

The social worker, a woman with long hair and glasses who'd been assigned to us, the one who gave me a pack of new underwear because I'd forgotten to pack them and who made sure Kenny got his dialysis, must have shown up at some point that night. She took me aside and said that she'd explain it all to the parents. This was her job; she could do this for me.

"No," I said. "These are my friends. These are kids that I know. They need to hear it from me." I swallowed hard. "And

Molly's *my* Molly. I get to tell her story."

And so, I gathered the kids and their parents together, with Gracie, and I stood there and explained it all. I was stepping out of myself, something I was so good at. I watched myself, making an announcement like the schoolteacher I was trained to be. I explained what had happened to Molly's brain because of the tumor, that it was damaged beyond repair. When I was done, I asked if anyone had any questions and one girl raised her hand. "I just have one," she said. "How long until Molly wakes up?" You could have heard a pin drop. I quietly said, "She is never going to wake up, Molly is gone."

As the group of girls fell apart, I noticed a man slipping into the back of the room. It was Greg. His son, David, was one of Molly's friends. He'd been there earlier in the day.

When I finished talking, I turned to him and asked, "Did you forget something?"

"No, I got to exit 11 and I heard a loud voice. I thought that maybe I'd fallen asleep while I was driving or something. Anyway, the voice told me that something had happened and that I should turn around." He took a breath. "So, I came back."

Greg is one of life's huggers. He's just there for people: his big, soft, fleshy body, his arms as vast as an ocean, ready to receive anyone who needs him. The reason he came back that night was just to stand there in the hallway, to hand out hugs to all those girls and their mothers, to me and Gracie. I remember noticing how wet his sweatshirt was from all the crying. And then, he got back in his car and headed home.

Like with Chaz, my old boyfriend, being Molly's nurse, Greg turning his car around that night was evidence to me of the universe working. Which is a hard thing to get your head around. Because if I believe that it's working to help me, that it's there to bring Chaz to be Molly's nurse and that it's there to turn Greg's car around, then I must believe that it somehow orchestrated Molly's death too. That it let her die. That it did both. That it took Molly away. And then it helped us survive her death.

At the end of my talk that night to the dance girls and their parents, Gracie stepped forward and said, "You'll all get a chance to say goodbye. I'll come with you to see Molly."

And that's what she did. While Greg gave out his hugs and I stood outside talking to the parents of the girls who stayed, Gracie took her friends by the hand and led them to Molly and told them that it was OK to touch her, to kiss her, to say their goodbyes.

In the moment of Molly's death, Gracie changed. In one of those strange, dark moments that mothers have when they look at their kids and fear the worst, that something might happen to one of them, I remember telling myself that if one of them had to go, it would be better if it were Gracie. Not because I loved her any less. But because Molly was the stronger one. Or so I thought. Molly would cope better without her than Gracie would without Molly.

Now I know that's not true.

We underestimate our children. Sometimes, we don't know them at all.

Later, the nurses would tell me, tears swimming in their eyes, that they'd never seen anything like it: Gracie taking care of her friends like that, when she was the one who'd lost everything.

At roughly 8:00 p.m. Gracie had found out that Molly had died.

By 10:00 p.m., she was helping her friends through their grief, she was holding their hands as they said goodbye to Molly.

Gracie and Molly had always been two halves of a whole, as close as twins, and although Molly was two years younger, she'd always been the dominant half. The stronger one. The one who held it all together. Without Molly, Gracie was in the dark. Or that's what we thought.

As it turned out, Gracie was stronger than any of us ever knew.

Chapter 10
Bargaining

By the time all the visitors had left, it was almost midnight. Gracie and Kenny went to David's House; I lay in the bed beside Molly. I thought of her friends taking that long drive home with their parents processing the news of Molly's death. Their lives would be changed forever. They had seen death up close. They knew that it could happen to any of them, anyone they loved, at any time. That this could happen to their sweet friend, Molly, who danced with them on the stage under the bright lights. I was meant to process the news of her death, too, that night. But as I looked at Molly, her sweet face, her head all bandaged up, I couldn't.

I just stared at her, willing her to wake up: *Please, Molly. Please, Molly. Please prove them wrong. Please wake up.* I spent the night bargaining with Molly. With the universe. Isn't it strange? Even after everything, after all the hours in the ER, after that doctor telling us it was too late, after the hours in surgery on Monday and her surgeon's hopeful words when Molly responded so well to the operation and then his tears at the MRI, the constant roller coaster of hopes dashed and raised and then the final announcement: Molly was dead. She was never going to wake up. Even after all this, I still begged: *Please wake up, Molly. Please wake up.*

I couldn't have slept for more than ten minutes that night.

I was too busy praying for her to come back.

It's been seven years now, and I don't think I'll ever stop praying for that.

Chapter 11
Not Another Moira

From the moment I was told that Molly wasn't coming back to us, I knew with a great sense of clarity that I didn't want her death to be kept silent. I didn't want her final days to be hidden or private or for people to find out about her death through word of mouth or a newspaper article. I wanted anyone who had come into contact with Molly's brief and beautiful life to have the chance to say goodbye.

One of the reasons I did this was because of Moira, my best friend in fourth grade. One day she was there at school, right beside me, and then she was gone. I loved her and I never got to say goodbye.

It was a different time. In the '70s, children were kept in the dark about most things. There was a thick curtain drawn between the world of childhood and the adult world. There were so many secrets. Perhaps the grown-ups saw this secrecy as a form of protection; they didn't want to hurt our young feelings or give us too much to carry. The truth was that it didn't protect us or ease our burdens; it made us feel scared and powerless and angry for being kept in the dark. We have learned, rightly, to be much more open with our children. To trust that the truth is always better in the long run than a cover-up.

Moira didn't come back for ages. Weeks passed and then months.

I remember asking my mom whether I could call her and say hi, but she said that we should wait to hear from Moira.

I remember feeling so detached from her. And at the same time, as I looked at her empty desk, as I spent recess alone, I missed her. And I didn't know what to do to get her back.

She didn't come back for the rest of the school year.

That summer, I bumped into her by chance as I was riding my bike home from summer school. It felt like I was seeing a ghost. I went straight over to her to say hi. We visited all morning. We picked up right where we left off. It felt so, so good to see her.

I walked her back home, pushing my green bike alongside her. She lifted her T-shirt and proudly showed me her scars. She said that she had had a tumor in her stomach. I remember looking wide-eyed at the long, jagged line that ran between her chest and her belly button. And there were horizontal lines too. Like someone had drawn a huge zipper down her torso.

She must have sensed my horror.

"It's OK," she said. "Now that the tumor's been taken out, I'm going to get better. The doctor said I should go for walks to build up my strength. Maybe you can come with me."

We made plans to walk again. I'd help her get strong and then after the summer Moira would come back to school and we'd be best friends again, play kickball at recess, and forget all about those strange weeks and months when she dropped out of my life.

It was the last time I ever saw Moira.

The tumor she'd had was cancerous. It killed her. I found out about her death when my friend Terri showed me her obituary in the newspaper. When I saw it, I broke down in tears. If I'd known that Moira was dying, I'd have tried harder to see her, to help her. To say goodbye, at least. As I think back to her cheerful words about getting better and coming back to school, I wonder if even she was kept in the dark about the fact that she was dying.

I yelled at my mother, an OR nurse who had taken part in some of Moira's operations, for not telling me what was happening.

"Moira's family wanted it to be kept secret," she said. "We had to respect their privacy."

But that just felt like an excuse to me. I was so devastated that I wasn't told that she was dying and that I wasn't given the chance to say goodbye.

A week later, I walked to her funeral with two of our friends, Terri and Jill. We wore our first-day-of-school dresses. We watched Moira's white casket being carried past us down the aisle of the church. It was closed, so we didn't even get to see her face.

She was buried on the far side of a cemetery near the prison. It would be almost twenty years before I would see her grave. I was walking with some of my students through the cemetery my first year teaching. Seeing her name on the stone brought me to my knees. All of the sadness, anger, and grief came rushing back. It was like no time had passed at all. I was glad that my students could witness that, that I could open up about what happened to Moira by talking to them about it.

Fifth grade started without Moira and eventually, I thought of her less and less. I made new best friends. Looking back, I'm shocked by how easy it was for her to disappear and for us all to move on.

It was Moira's story that made it clear to me that there would be no secrecy around Molly's death and that anyone who wanted to find out what had happened to her and anyone who wanted to say goodbye would be given the chance to do just that.

In those days, when I invited the world to come and spend time with Molly, I was interviewed by the local TV station. They asked me how I had it in me to be so generous, to give the little time I had left with Molly to others. I replied that she didn't really belong to me.

"She's at an age when I drop her off at school in the morning at 8:30 and sometimes I don't see her again until 8:30 at night," I explained to the interviewer. "And in those hours when she wasn't with me, she was somebody's student and somebody's best friend and somebody's dancer and somebody's sister. She wasn't mine during all those hours. And to keep her from the people who loved her when she's leaving feels selfish to me."

But it was more than that too. It was because of Moira. I didn't want Molly to slip away like Moira had. Or to be forgotten. Or for her friends to feel betrayed because no one told them what had happened to her. I needed to invite the world in to say goodbye. It was my way of fighting against the secrecy of my childhood. Of righting the wrong of the way Moira's death had been handled. And it was also my way of surviving. I understand that some families—and some mothers—have a profound need for privacy. I've lost count of the number of times people have asked me how I managed it—having so many people around, being so public about everything. The truth is that I needed people and their support. How could I not? How could I just sit there alone and stare at Molly as life seeped out of her?

Having shared that dark time with so many continues to help me today. Knowing that we didn't go through it alone. That Molly didn't just disappear.

Death is hard anyway. The death of a child even harder. The sudden and unexplained death of a child harder still. No one was expecting Molly to die. They had a right to be given an explanation and a chance to say goodbye. To be part of her legacy. And I needed to see the world say goodbye to her because it was an acknowledgment that she'd been part of all our lives, that she'd mattered and that something terrible had happened to her, something that was not OK, and that now she was gone.

Chapter 12
A Thousand Goodbyes

On Wednesday morning, I called the three public schools that Molly, Gracie, and I were so closely attached to and told them what had happened and that I wanted anyone who felt a connection to Molly, whoever they were, to have a chance to say goodbye.

It's been my mission through all this to pull something good from what happened to Molly.

Some days, that mission feels pointless when, in the end, all I want is to have her back. But I know Molly would have wanted her death to count for something, just like her life had. And to be honest, working to bring some good from the tragedy of Molly's death is what helps me survive.

I wanted her organs to be taken to save other lives. I was so angry when that wasn't possible. Now, I wanted these children and families who loved Molly to have the chance to say goodbye properly. I didn't want them to be left with questions and a vacuum. I wanted them to have closure and to engage with death in a way that modern life doesn't allow for, especially with young people. For many of these kids, Molly would be their first encounter with death. I wanted it to be an encounter that deepened them as human beings, that helped them. I wanted it to spur conversations with their parents about what it meant to be alive and how to cherish every moment.

And how to cope with the death of someone they loved when inevitably it came.

Every one of those children had to face the trauma of Molly's sudden disappearance from their lives. They deserved better.

At the time, I couldn't have articulated this wish so clearly, but looking back now, I know that the reason I made all those phone calls, the reason I didn't just close the door to Molly's hospital room and ask for us to be left alone with our grief, was because I wanted to do something good when all the rest had been taken out of my hands. A few parents have thanked me for that, that I gave their children an experience of death that was positive, one that formed their blueprint for coping with death for the rest of their lives. That they could face it head-on, that they could see it and touch it, and that they could survive it. More than survive it, it could make them stronger.

The nurses emptied the room next to Molly's so that we would have more space for visitors. Then they prepared her. They removed her bandages. They shampooed and braided her hair. They brushed her teeth. And the whole time, they spoke to her, telling her what they were doing. They were kind and gentle. It didn't matter that she was dead; she was still their patient.

Here, I saw how amazing medical professionals could be. The kindness with which that doctor had explained to Gracie that Molly wasn't going to wake up. The care and respect with which these nurses washed Molly's dead body.

I took a washcloth and passed it over Molly's soft, translucent skin. And I thought about Kenny and all the baths he'd given her and Gracie. He was the bath guy. He always made it fun for them.

At the time Gracie was born, Kenny was working over fifty hours a week away from home, filling vending machines all over New Hampshire. But when he was home, he pulled his weight, and he was always there for his girls.

When Gracie was a tiny baby, I'd hear him singing to her

as he bathed her. Doing bath time was his way of giving me a break but he loved it and he was so good at it. I'd hear tiny squeals of laughter and splashing.

My fondest memory of the two of them was on Gracie's second birthday. Molly had been born twenty-three days earlier, and Gracie was struggling with the adjustment of having a little sister and needing to share her parents' attention. So, we threw her a big birthday party to make her feel special. By the end of the day, Gracie was overwhelmed and tired and covered in cake and sobbing her eyes out. I was nursing Molly upstairs, so Kenny took care of Gracie. I remember walking downstairs to the bathroom off the kitchen, where I found Gracie lying on her back in the tub. Kenny was leaning over her, singing "Happy Birthday," so softly it sounded like a lullaby. Slowly and gently, he washed her arms and her legs, still singing. She was still whimpering but you could tell that her nervous system was calming down from his voice and his touch. I thought about how lucky I was to have married a man who was such a good father, a truth that hasn't changed, even through all our marital ups and downs. That memory of Gracie and Kenny will stay with me forever.

And then Molly got old enough to get in the bathtub with Gracie and the whole bathroom turned into a monsoon. There was water everywhere. Kenny would get out of his work clothes and put on a pair of running shorts and a T-shirt and by the time bath time was over, he was soaked. But he loved it. And he always made it fun. Colored bubbles and bath toys and tile crayons and songs and stories. Molly would get out early, always the more impatient one, and walk around naked for a while, clutching a book. Gracie stayed in a bit longer. But it was always their special time—the three of them.

When they were too big to take baths together, Kenny taught them to take their first showers and to wash their own hair. He always showed up.

Affection from fathers to their children is so utterly important in raising healthy, happy men and women. Kenny got that. He was ahead of his time. And I don't take it for granted, not for a second.

My mind shifted back to the present and I looked at Molly lying on the hospital bed. She looked clean and beautiful with her hair washed.

Bethany, one of our close family friends whose daughter was a dear friend of Molly and Gracie, came home early from her vacation. She tied Molly's hair into a bun and wrapped it in a pink ribbon.

And then it began. The long, long hours and days of good-byes.

Since Molly's death, I've become part of several online grief groups. I've learned of the many, horrifying ways in which parents can lose their children and I've learned that I'm in the lucky category when it comes to having a dead child.

Don't get me wrong. There is no good way to lose a child. But I'm grateful for this: we had time. That between Molly's actual death at our local hospital at 1:30 a.m. on Monday, May 2 to when she was unplugged on Saturday at lunchtime, she was never alone. As her soul was transitioning, she was sur-rounded by people she loved and who loved her. Those people got to say goodbye. And I got to say goodbye.

~

All through that Wednesday, the visitors came.

Molly's teachers from elementary school, from middle school. Her classmates. I'd pleaded with the school to give anyone who wanted it time off to come and say goodbye. The kids Molly had played in the orchestra with. The kids she'd been on stage with recently in her performance of *Bye Bye Birdie*. The kids who she sat next to in class. The kids who she looked out for because they didn't fit in.

People came for me too. Like the girls from my cross-country team at a local high school. Four of my best friends from high school. My college roommates.

Jenna, the wife of DJ Nazzy, a local celebrity, came and took off her "May the force be with you" *Star Wars* T-shirt and gave it to Molly to wear, because it was the fourth of May and because she believed, like everyone, that despite our words about Molly's death that maybe some force would swoop down and bring her back to life. That would make more sense than her never coming back. Many of her dance and theatre friends came again and again.

Derek, one of Molly's closest friends, came every day. They had a special relationship, doing homework together over Face-Time and talking about everything. A week before, they'd had a disagreement and Derek was heartbroken that Molly might be mad at him. This wasn't how it was meant to be. They were meant to have another hundred fights and to make up and get closer each time in the way that the closest friends ever do. They were meant to grow up together. I could feel his grief for a life without Molly.

The head of Molly's dance school, Miss Cindy, came several times too. She kept squeezing Molly's hands, certain that she'd wake up. When it finally hit her that Molly was dead, she fell to her knees in the hallway and sobbed. Like all of us, she didn't understand why Molly had been taken from us.

"Raise your hand if Molly was ever mean to you," she called out to the dance girls, desperate at how unfair all this was.

As a joke, Gracie raised her hand. There were no two people closer than Gracie and Molly, but in family life, we hurt each other. Molly could be mean to us, though that was only because we were so close. To the rest of the world, she only ever showed kindness.

No. Besides Gracie's, not a hand went up.

"Not many of us can die claiming that!" Cindy boomed.

Watching all those hundreds of people who came to say goodbye to Molly—and hearing what they said about her—it began to dawn on me that my little girl's short life had had greater impact than I ever realized. That lesson was going to go even deeper in the next few days.

Chapter 13
Gracie's Decision

When the Wednesday visitors from the day left, Charlene called us in for another meeting.

Another meeting.

I would come to hate those meetings. I felt in my gut, every time she asked us to come together, that she was about to say something to make our situation even worse. Another blow, one more thing that my heart and mind and body couldn't cope with in the unfolding story of Molly's death. She was just doing her job. She was following the rules. I shouldn't blame her. But no one should be called in for *meetings* to discuss the details of their child's death.

What's she going to tell us now? I remember thinking. But then it hit me that she couldn't tell us anything worse. Molly was dead. In a week or so, she'd be lying in the cold ground. There was nothing left to say, was there?

Kenny and I left Gracie with her friends and went to talk to Charlene.

When we were all settled in the room, Charlene said, "We need to talk about unplugging Molly from life support."

~

Until now, we hadn't really had a sense of the hospital's plans for Molly or when her life would officially end. Somehow, this hadn't factored into our thinking, that there would be an end point for us to decide on. I suppose that all the visitors had distracted us from the practical realities of her death. That there'd be an end point to all these goodbyes.

"But you said there was no rush, that we could take as long as we needed to say goodbye," I stammered.

"The body on life support is tricky to maintain," Charlene said.

"What does that mean?" Her words weren't making any sense to me. What did it matter when we unplugged Molly?

"It's not good to keep someone who's died on life support for too long," Charlene explained. "It puts too great a strain on the body."

I still didn't get what she was saying. Molly was dead; what more strain could be put on her body? I didn't want to be having his meeting or having to think about this.

Looking back now at all the photos we'd taken over that week, I realize that Charlene had a point. You could see it. As the hours and the days passed. Molly's mouth hung open a bit more. Her eyelids no longer stayed fully closed. The Molly we saw at the end of the week wasn't the Molly who'd been brought into the children's hospital on Monday. She wanted us to respect her body and the dying process and maybe protect us, too, from the distress of seeing her getting worse.

But still, it was a surprise. What Charlene was saying to us. What she was asking us to decide.

"I work on Fridays but then I'm off for the weekend," Charlene said gently. "I'd like to be there for the procedure."

I'd never warmed much to Charlene. I had no complaints about how she did her job, we just didn't connect on a personal level. And I was touched that she wanted to be there. But her presence wasn't a priority for me.

"So, I think Friday would be a good day to unplug Molly,"

she added, pressing us to agree.

To *unplug* Molly. What an ugly word, I thought. You don't unplug a human being. You don't unplug a child. And anyway, I wasn't ready.

"We need more time. There are still so many people who want to say goodbye—"

"I don't think we should draw this out," Charlene said.

We sat in silence for a while. It hit me that there was going to be an end point to all of this. You'd have thought I'd have got there by now. That I understood that Molly was dead and that, one day, we'd be leaving the hospital without her. But there are so many parts to the process of letting a child go, and now I was being told that there was one more I had to face, to decide on. The time when the machines that kept my child's body alive – the oxygen that allowed her to breathe, the ventilator that kept her blood pumping – would have to be switched off.

When Charlene left, I went to find Gracie to explain to her what was happening.

Gracie had always been a compliant child. She had her moments of rebellion like any kid but, generally speaking, she went along with our decisions. It was Molly who challenged and questioned me. Gracie was gentle. She deferred to my judgment. More than that, she trusted me.

But not today. Today, as I watched her responding to my words, I saw a look rush across her face. The flash of an emotion so strong I felt I could reach out and touch it. I saw the anger go from one side to the other. I saw the shift in her eyes. I felt her body go rigid beside me.

"No!" she said.

I explained to her what Charlene had said to us. About us needing to be respectful of her sister's body, about how it was under strain.

But again, Gracie said no.

Many of the visitors who hadn't had the chance to say goodbye were Gracie's friends. We needed the extra day. And

Friday felt too soon.

I'd never seen her so angry.

"No!" she said, over and over again. "We need the Friday."

I stepped in.

"Gracie's right," I said. "We should wait until Saturday."

I could sense Charlene's disapproval. Kenny went with me because he knew I was putting Gracie first.

For a whole number of reasons, it turned out that it was the right decision to wait an extra day. In some ways, I wish we'd waited even longer, long enough to see whether Molly had cancer so we could donate her organs. Molly would have liked that, to know that her death had helped a whole ton of people. I still regret that sometimes. But the personal reason we needed more time was because there were more people who needed to say goodbye. *We* needed more time to say goodbye.

And it happened that Chaz, my boyfriend from twenty-three years ago, was working on Saturday. That he would be there to unplug Molly. Someone I'd loved and dated for two years, long, long before Molly's life was even a possibility, would help us go through one of the hardest parts of this process.

The people who are around you when you're saying good-bye to your child can make the moment survivable. I needed him there.

There were several times that week when I watched Gracie grow up. On Tuesday night, when she told her friends that Molly was never going to wake up again. And now, on Wednesday, when she wanted to be the one to decide when her sister—her other half, so close she may as well have been a twin—should be unplugged.

Gracie won that battle. The first of many she would have to face in this long journey of grief.

~

Because of Gracie and the extra time she fought for, the last good-byes were some of the most precious and moving. Another bus driver came. Brenda, a second-grade teacher who loved Molly. She sat at her bedside and thanked her for being such a kind, curious, enthusiastic student. Skylar, a best friend who hadn't heard that Molly was sick, was able to come in with her mother, holding a Vermont Teddy bear with Molly's name on it. An aunt who had lost her son to a brain tumor when he was eight said goodbye through FaceTime because she was too far away to come in. More dance and school friends. And a small, skinny-legged boy holding a "Get Well Soon" balloon who, ignored by his peers, had been picked out by Molly to work on a project with her. His mother told me that he was in love with her.

As I watched him standing there, clutching his "Get Well Soon" balloon, my heart broke. It broke for how it wasn't just me who was losing Molly, Xander was losing her too. Hundreds of people were losing her, the girl who saw it as her purpose in life to make them happy.

And because of Gracie, Molly got to have her first and last kiss from a boy she'd likely have fallen in love with. A tender moment, one of the many times I realized that.

It was Gracie who brought him into Molly's room to say goodbye.

As he leaned over her body, the girl he'd danced with and acted with on stage and spent years with as a best friend, tears dropped from his eyes and then, lightly, he kissed her goodbye.

For both, I believe, it was their first kiss.

For Molly, it was her last kiss as well.

I cried for her, watching that moment, knowing how much this boy meant to Molly, and how this was just one in a long list of beautiful futures she was going to miss.

This future grief is perhaps the hardest part of child loss. You don't just mourn who they were but who they might have become.

This truth began to dawn on me that week as I watched Molly's young friends saying goodbye to her. The realization that it wouldn't just be the memories that we'd have with Molly that would haunt us but also the memories she'd never get to make.

She'd never get to experience having a boyfriend. She wouldn't get to do the school projects, which she'd have aced. She wouldn't dance next to her friends whom she'd trained with for so many years. The concerts, in which she should have played her violin, would go on without her. The curtain would rise on the theatre productions she'd never be in. She told me, just a few weeks before, after her performance in *Bye, Bye, Birdie*, that she felt she'd found her people and her home. That the theatre was where she most wanted to be.

It's been six years as I write this, and still, the beginning of the school year gets to me. My mom friends are posting pictures on Facebook of their high school seniors starting. Those were the twelve- and thirteen-year-olds who were Molly's friends before she died. Her school friends and dance friends and gymnastic friends and just the friends she picked up along the way because she was Molly. They felt sophisticated and grown up, but to us, they were still little kids then. Some of the girls hadn't hit puberty yet. Some of the boys hadn't had their voices break yet. But now I look at these pictures and I see adults. I see long-limbed, young adults with confident smiles and heads held high with a knowledge of who they want to be in the world and a certainty that they will be in the world. This year, they will make decisions about their futures and prepare to leave school and home. And Molly, my Molly, is still lying in her coffin, frozen at thirteen, and I don't know what do with this knowledge that weighs on me: I haven't just lost the Molly that was but also the Molly that will be. That I haven't just lost the amazing kid she was but all the future iterations too. Senior Molly. Graduating Molly. College student Molly. Fall-in-love-hard Molly. Get-her-first-job Molly. Getting-married Molly. Having-kids Molly. Travel-the-world Molly. Or do-none-of-those-things Molly and tread her own path, which, most likely, she would have done.

There are a hundred lives that Molly never got to live. And I get to imagine them all, knowing that she's never coming back.

Chapter 14
Who She Really Was

*Most parents don't really know
their children.
- Otto Frank*

I'd never get to see the Molly that could have been. But that week, with every visitor who came in and out of Molly's room, I was given a gift that I had never expected to receive: I came to find out who my daughter really was. And that was the true miracle.

~

Four days before Molly died, I'd sat in the Anne Frank Museum in Amsterdam, listening to Otto Frank talking about his daughter. He said how close they were and how much they had shared; he believed he knew his daughter. It was only after she died and he read her diary that he came to understand that there was so much more to his little girl than he could ever have imagined.

Anne Frank died when she was fifteen. Molly when she was thirteen. It turns out that they were both strangers—as we all are perhaps—to those who loved them most.

Looking back, I see signs that my body and my mind were

preparing me for Molly's death long before she was admitted to the ER.

Sitting in the Anne Frank Museum was one of those signs. Otto Frank's words were a sign. I felt a kind of awakening when I heard him talking about his daughter and as I read quotations from him on the wall. I sat there, crying, longing to get back to my Gracie and Molly. I didn't know then that at the exact moment when I was listening to Otto Frank and having those gut-wrenching feelings, Molly was on the bathroom floor vomiting profusely and that she would visit the pediatrician's office later with Kenny because her headaches were becoming unbearable. Our babies' umbilical cords might be cut at birth but it's my belief that their bodies are forever connected to our own.

I was sobbing in that museum while she was in pain. I was sobbing, perhaps, because I knew that soon I'd be in the same position as Otto Frank: having to survive without my child.

It took me an entire day and a text conversation with Molly to snap out of that feeling of panic and dread. To be honest, it never fully left me. I needed to get back to her, to hold her, to make sure she was OK. Otto Frank had missed out on his daughter, he'd lost his child. I would use his story to make sure that I didn't miss another moment of Molly's life. That's what I told myself as I left the museum that day. It turned out that a few days later, Otto Frank's words would hit much closer to home.

On the one hand, Molly and I were profoundly alike. Sharp. Articulate. Stubborn as hell. Both of us believed we were right about everything. Our feelings ran deep. We struggled because of these similarities. It's not an unusual scenario between mothers and daughters, to be so close that just by living alongside each other, we knock into and bruise each other.

Part of my future grief for Molly is that I won't see a version of myself growing up. And by that, I mean I won't see the bits that were so like me going through all those milestones:

falling in and out of love, graduating from high school, finding her passion in life and seeing it through, going up the hills and down into the valleys of being alive in the world. I was so excited to see Molly grow up. It felt like I'd be watching a part of myself living all over again, only doing it better this time. Maybe, I thought, she would get things right in a way that I hadn't.

But this thinking suggests that I knew her completely and as Otto Frank said, and as I now understand for myself, we know very little about the inner lives of our children.

Everything about parenthood is a paradox, and this is no exception. On the one hand, we feel completely responsible for who our children are and who they become. If we're able to have our own biological children, they're a genetic extension of us. We grow our little humans from seed. They live in our bellies for nine months. And, for the rest of their childhood (and of all animals, the process of parenting for humans is the longest), we nurture them into being.

And so, we assume a deep knowledge of our children.

But in truth, they are as much strangers as they are familiar.

There is a part of them that is and always will stand apart from us. That was the discovery Otto Frank made when he read Anne's diaries after her death. He says that it was a miracle that the diary was saved and so a miracle that he got to know this side of her. It turned out that I, too, was given a miracle that would allow me to get to know my little stranger. Not a diary, but five days when the world came to tell me about her.

Molly's brain tumor ruptured in the middle of Sunday night at our local hospital. That is where Molly's journey could have ended. If she'd been someone my age, it *would* have ended then. The doctors wouldn't have bothered to call in the neurological surgeon from out of town or to take her to the children's hospital to see whether, by removing the tumor, they might just be able to get her to wake up again. The chances were so slim that they wouldn't risk it on anyone other than a little girl. Anyway, her journey and our knowledge of her would have ended in the pediatric ward of our hospital. But by some miracle, the doctors agreed to transfer her, to give her one last chance, and it was because of that decision that we were given another five days with Molly, days that allowed me to find out who my daughter really was.

There's something about people who die young. Looking back at Molly's life and knowing what I know now about the impact she had on others—and thinking about Anne Frank too—I wonder whether somehow the universe allows those who are with us for only a short time to lead brighter, deeper, more connected lives. This was something that Otto Frank recognized, reading his daughter's diary. And it was something I found out about Molly in the days after she died as people poured in to see Molly and every single one of them had a story to share about who she was and what she'd meant to them. Nothing could have prepared me for what I heard.

In the fog of grief and exhaustion and overwhelmingness that was that week, there are some stories that stayed with me.

There was a girl who came up with her parents to say goodbye to Molly. She was a school friend. Her parents told me how Molly was the only reason she was OK at school.

And so, my knowledge of my little girl deepened. I began to see her as she really was. It turned out that I'd hardly known her at all.

Mr. John, the custodian at Molly's elementary school, took the morning off to say goodbye to Molly. Most of the visitors had left by then and he'd decided not to come with the rest of the staff because he wanted to see Molly on his own. So, it was just him, me, and Molly.

We sat in the window seat, and he put his face in his hands and choked out his words. He was utterly devastated.

I asked him why he'd come. Why Molly meant so much to him.

"She just took care of everybody," he sobbed.

He was a grown man in his late fifties, sitting there, crying for a little girl who had taken the trouble to notice him.

"You know, we're the invisible people," he said.

I remember when Gracie and Molly were little, I'd talk to them about my coaching or my teaching and I'd always say: *The more money you make, the less important you are. Sure, the principal has an important job, but it's the custodians and the bus drivers and the teaching assistants and the cooks and the secretaries, those employees are the important ones in the schools. They take care of everything and make sure it works. Without them, the school couldn't run.*

I told Molly and Gracie that it was their job to be kind and to say hello and to call the custodians by their names. Gracie was never unkind to anybody, but she was timid and so often stayed quiet. Molly was different. She intuited all of this. It turned out that she took my words and acted on them in ways that I could never have dreamed of.

"Being invisible means we see everything," Mr. John explained. "We see kids pushing other kids and ramming into us. We see kids spit out their gum on the floor and we have to clean that up. And we're ignored. People walk past and say nothing. But Molly never, ever walked by without saying hello and asking how I was. And she never forgot to thank me. And then I'd watch her when she thought I wasn't looking, and I'd see her hang up the coats that had fallen off their hooks and neaten up the boots, and then she'd run into a little kindergartener who was confused and she'd take him to where he needed to go." He choked back another sob. "I never saw a child so kind. I can't understand why, if there's a God, he'd take her."

This was one of my Otto Frank moments. I sat there listening to Mr. John talking and crying and seeing how wrecked he was and how he couldn't get his head around what had happened to Molly.

As I hugged Mr. John goodbye and watched him walk away,

I remember a conversation I'd had with him when I cleaned out Molly's locker at the end of fifth grade. I saw nine thousand mints stacked up on her shelf. Mr. John walked by, and I stopped to show him the locker.

"Do you know where all these mints came from?" I asked.

He smiled. "From me."

"Do you give mints to all the kids?" I asked.

"No," he said. "The only person I give mints to is Molly."

"Why?" I asked.

"Because she just always takes care of everybody. I wanted her to know that I appreciated that."

I should have guessed then what an impact Molly had on people's lives, but it took her death for me to see the full extent of it.

Paul, Molly's fifth-grade teacher, took the day off teaching and stayed for a whole day. He just hung out and helped me and spent time with Molly. He was devastated by her death.

When she was in kindergarten and she was so smart, I told Paul that she'd want him as her fifth-grade teacher because she could learn so much from him. He was good with bright kids.

"What can I do to help, Barb?" he kept asking.

I was a wreck that day. Tiredness was catching up with me. I'd been managing so many people and I was still trying to take in what was going on with Molly. "Just sit with Molly," I said. "Just be with her. And when people come in, help them be with her too."

So, he sat there for hours. He talked to her. He talked to Gracie. He managed the visitors.

At *MollyB the Musical*, a memorial we held for her a few weeks after she died, Paul spoke about what an incredible student she'd been and mentioned her essay on Malala Yousafzai. Molly was drawn to people like Malala, those who'd overcome the odds, who sacrificed their lives for others.

Re-reading Molly's essay now, the poignancy of a girl standing up for the rights of other young girls is not lost on me.

Malala once said, "I tell my story, not because it is unique, but because it is the story of many girls."

I believe that if Molly had survived, she would have been an advocate for young girls and women, like Malala. For their rights to be heard and seen.

That's why she wrote about Malala. Because these are things she believed in.

I wish I could talk to Molly about it all now. About her and Malala. About how much more work there is to be done until we're all equal. Molly would have been an activist, I'm sure of it. In her own way, she was already.

Paul went on to say he'd never taught anyone like her.

I didn't know any of this. How much Molly meant to him and to so many other kids and teachers and members of the support staff. She'd been living right under my nose and sure, I knew she was a smart kid and that she felt things deeply and that she tried to be kind but I didn't know the detail. I didn't know the hundreds of things she did, big and small, day in, day out, to make people's lives better, whoever they were.

Chris, Molly's seventh-grade science teacher also came on Thursday. He showed up in a sparkling, colorful lab coat saying that he thought it was so bright and shiny and funny that it might snap her into waking up. It hadn't sunk in for him yet—I don't think that it had sunk in for anyone who visited her that week in the hospital, that she wasn't coming back. That neither prayer nor healings nor even the brightest, craziest, funniest jacket in the whole wide world would make Molly open her eyes again.

Chris told me about how, one lunchtime at school, Molly came to see him in his classroom. She said that she hated the cafeteria and asked whether she could eat her lunch with him.

"I'm afraid you can't do that," he said.

He watched her heart sink.

"But if you want to start a lunch club, I'll be your advisor," he added quickly, smiling.

They started up the club with four kids. Every kid who signed up had to have a two-day trial period to make sure they behaved. It was an honor to be in lunch club and they needed to show that they recognized that by how they acted when they were there. By the time Molly died, lunch club had sixty members. It became a safe space for kids who didn't fit in with the popular group and who found eating in the cafeteria tough. For some, it was the part of the school day that they looked forward to most.

A week or so before she died, Molly changed the bio on her Instagram account. She wrote:

> *Do you think you have a purpose?*
> *If so, what?*
> *I think mine is to make people happy.*
> *Does that make you happy?*
> *Yes?*
> *Purpose Fulfilled.*

The words chill me now. How much my thirteen-year-old wanted to make the world better. And how, in some strange way, she saw that purpose as fulfilled. I wish I had asked her more about those last two words. But the other words, I understood those, I knew what she meant by them and how they worked themselves out in her life.

Happy has become a bit of a buzzword now. I imagine that Molly would roll her eyes at it a bit, how everyone is trying to find ways to make themselves happy. That wasn't what happiness meant to her. For her, finding ways to make people happy had to do with justice and fairness and goodness and righting the wrongs of life.

What bothered Molly forever was that kids got things that made them happy or were rewarded for things they did, but sometimes the reason they could do those things was because they had money or attentive parents or parents at all or they weren't hyperactive or had a different skin color. Molly would notice. In terms of her wanting to make people happy, we all talked about it—me, Gracie, and Kenny—Molly just wanted things to be fair. She didn't want anyone to be left out. She never wanted anyone to be judged for things they couldn't control. Everything she did: winning the scooter for Habaku, Raina's recess reading club, the Easter basket for Deepseka, lunch club. She couldn't stand seeing anyone left out or suffering for something they hadn't done. If someone was a jerk or a bully, she cut them off. She always, always, always vied for the underdog.

Molly understood happiness in a way that was deep and complex and beautiful. And when she found unhappiness and suffering, she transformed it.

In the years since Molly died, I've watched the world begin to change. The rise of the #metoo movement and #blacklivesmatter and a greater awareness of the brutal inequalities and deeply ingrained prejudices in our society. I wonder how she would have survived this time. I think I know. With the deeper knowledge of Molly that her teachers gave me, I know that this is how she would have experienced it:

First, it would have gone deep. It would have upset her and kept her up at night and left her feeling utterly helpless. And angry too. But then, one day, she would have got up, wiped her tears, brushed herself off, and worked out a way to help. She would have been an activist like Malala, whom she wrote about, or Greta Thunberg or Anne Frank. She would have found a way to speak to the injustices of our times. Perhaps, through her death, she has.

The kids Molly helped will carry her with them for the rest of their lives.

A few weeks after her funeral, Chris invited me to visit the lunch club and to share a pizza with them. *Molly did all this,* I thought, looking out at all those kids.

Like Paul, Chris was angry too. "Why did Molly have to be taken?" he asked.

That's what I heard, over and over.

Why Molly?

There were other teachers who reached out later because they couldn't come to say goodbye in person. Like Miss Meredith, Molly's dance teacher, who started driving to the hospital and then turned around because she just couldn't face it.

Or Mrs. LaPlante, her sixth-grade science teacher who sent me the sweetest card saying how kind Molly was. A year before Molly started lunch club, she'd sit and have lunch with Mrs. LaPlante to avoid the popularity politics of the school cafeteria. Molly found out that her teacher liked licorice candy, so she went out of her way to find ones for her, and she'd bring them in as treats for their shared lunches. Marianne LaPlante wrote that she didn't understand why God took kids like Molly.

But that's the thing about death, isn't it? It doesn't interview its candidates. It doesn't pick people who are worthy of dying because they're mean or did bad things and let the kind ones stay on a bit longer. It just takes people, whoever they are. And we're left trying to work out why.

There's something else Otto Frank said in an interview shortly before he died in 1980:

I am almost ninety now and my strength is slowly fading. But the mission that Anne passed on keeps giving me new strength to fight for reconciliation and for human rights across the world.

The world presses grieving parents to move on, to become happy again, to invest in life rather than in death. I know that I have a journey of healing to go on, but remembering Molly and her death is not a form of staying stuck. Remembering Molly is a way of moving forward: as I draw strength from her life and her death, as Otto Frank did from his daughter's life and death, I'm inspired to keep fighting to make the world a better place.

Neither Molly nor Anne should have died. And they were both so close to surviving.

Anne Frank died two weeks before the liberation.

Molly's brain tumor was benign and easily operable.

If the war had ended earlier, Anne Frank would likely be alive today. If Molly's tumor had been caught earlier, she'd be with us now.

Anne Frank was a beautiful soul. Had she lived, she would no doubt have made a huge contribution to the world. But the good that's been done through her death and through her book and through her father's willingness to share her privacy is profound. Her death and her story changed humanity.

That's a huge motivator for me. Molly wasn't Anne Frank, but if we can tell her story and if we keep her spirit alive, kind spirit that always looked out for those who needed her most, if we make her familiar to people, even in her death, maybe we can make all this matter.

To a grieving mother the affirmation in Mr. Frank's statement about still gaining strength from his child forty years after her death is huge. Molly wasn't Anne Frank, but remembering his words about his daughter, I promise myself every day that I will use Molly's story to help others and to teach the world about her purpose here. This book is part of that promise.

Chapter 15

Proof of Death

At one point, in the blur of those last days before Molly was unplugged, the doctor in charge of Molly's case said we had to ask the visitors to step into the neighboring room that they'd set up for us. Molly had to undergo a special procedure that proved that she was legally dead.

This was another blow. I knew that the unplugging was coming, but I thought that was as bad as it was going to get, that there wasn't anything else we'd have to survive while we were in the hospital. And more than that, I didn't understand why we needed a procedure. Hadn't the doctors and nurses spent all week persuading me that Molly was dead, that there was nothing more we could?

Well, it turns out that the process of death isn't nearly as absolute as we imagine. For most it's not a case of being alive one moment and dead the next. It's a process. There's a gray area.

Charlene explained that this procedure would help us understand that Molly had really gone. And that it would help us come to terms with unplugging her the day after.

It was hard pushing our visitors out like that. I was constantly balancing our needs as a family with a profound longing that everyone who knew Molly and wanted to say goodbye should have some time with her. Some of our visitors went home. Others waited in the spare room next to Molly's.

Finally, it was just me, Kenny, and Gracie in the room with Molly.

Dr. G. came in with Molly's nurse and with Dennis, the case manager. He turned to Gracie and explained the process to her in the same soft, gentle voice he'd used when he told her that her sister wasn't going to wake up. He was so careful and kind and clear. It reminded me that there are good, competent doctors who see and listen and act with integrity.

"If this upsets you, it *should* upset you. We're trying to upset Molly too. If we can upset her enough for her to wake up, it means her body can wake up. If she doesn't respond, it means that her body has already stopped working and all these machines are doing is keeping her blood flowing and giving her oxygen to help her breathe until we decide what to do next."

In our state, when a person is under the age of eighteen, you must go to additional lengths to prove that a child is truly dead. In part, it's for legal reasons; no one wants to unplug the ventilator of a child who might still be alive. Another part of it is to help the families struggling with the prospect of letting go. If they see, clearly and definitely, that the child they love is gone, that their body is no longer able to respond, then—so it's argued—it's easier when it comes to remove them from life support.

And they were right. As horrifying as it was to watch, I understand now why they make families take part in this. I didn't realize it then, but I wouldn't have been able to follow through on the unplugging as easily if I hadn't watched this. She still seemed too alive, too much like she was still sleeping. I needed more persuading that she wasn't going to wake up.

"We're going to do some really mean things to Molly," Dr. G went on. "We're going to try and make her wake up. We're going to make her really mad."

The doctor kept apologizing. And the nurses on call too. To us. To Gracie, especially, who was still very young to be going through this. And then to Molly. That's what got to me most, how they talked to her, like she was still here. Like she could hear and feel everything that was going on.

"We're sorry, Molly," the doctor said. "You're going to be really mad at us for doing this ... but we have to do this ..."

And then we all stood in a circle as if a show was about to start and watched.

We watched as they poured ice cold water in Molly's ear, and she did nothing.

We watched as they held open one eye and then the other and rubbed it with a Q-tip, and she didn't flinch.

We watched as they pinched her sweet shoulder hard right by her neck, and she didn't move.

We watched as they took one of those reflex tools and rubbed it hard along the bottom of her foot, and she didn't react.

And we watched as they grabbed the skin by the side of her stomach and grabbed it hard, and, still, she did nothing.

As they went through the procedure, they recorded their voices into a machine, they read the numbers on the screens around Molly, they described her lack of response.

I remember wondering how a doctor first came up with this list of procedures. These ways of forcing someone to wake up or to check for sure that someone was dead. It felt more like something a spy would learn, a way to torture someone to get information than something a hospital would devise.

Every time they did something else, I wanted to scream, to yank their hands away, to tell them to stop. There is nothing more counterintuitive than a mother allowing someone to hurt their child. Just seeing them doing that to my sweet Molly made my body jolt and squirm. But Molly felt nothing. I guess that was the point.

So, I just stood there, holding Molly's hand, watching. Because I knew that they had to do this. To prove that she wasn't going to wake up. To prove that she was dead.

But also, because maybe, just maybe, she might wake up.

There were a few times in the procedure when it felt so unbearable to watch, I looked away. But mostly, I kept my eyes fixed on Molly. I needed to see if there was even the slightest tremor of a reaction in my little girl's body.

All three of us—me, Kenny and Gracie—we knew she wasn't going to wake up. But we willed her to wake up all the same. I think that, secretly, even the doctors and nurses who knew better than us that Molly's body had given up, were praying for a miracle too. Together, we prayed that she would blink or flinch or gasp. But she didn't move.

Because despite everything we'd been through and heard, we still believed that a miracle might happen. That she might still live.

This was my reality for that whole week.

Coming to terms with the fact, knowing in my heart of hearts, that Molly would never wake up.

And wishing that she would.

I know that she's not coming back. I know that she's buried deep in the cold ground of the cemetery a mile from my house. But still, I expect her to run up the porch steps and fly into the house and pick up her dance costume that's been hanging on the stair rail this whole time.

I know that if I were to dig her up and look at her body, there'd be hardly anything left now.

But still, I sometimes believe that she's not dead.

It's hard for anyone who loses someone they love deeply to let go of this hope. But it's hardest of all when you lose a child. As a mother, your brain and your heart and your body and your spirit and whatever else it is that makes up who you are isn't wired to live in a world where your child is dead.

I remember one of the first grief counselors I went to see after Molly died explaining it to me in a way that made absolute sense to me.

She explained how, from the moment a baby is conceived, a mother's neural pathways are forever changed, that she's forged to respond to the needs, to the aliveness of her child. Every kick and shift in the womb elicits a response. And the pathways and the responses grow stronger with every day of the pregnancy. By the time you've given birth, your child can be crying five miles away and your breasts will start leaking milk. The connection goes deep.

After thirteen years of living with your child, your brain is so deeply changed that it will never go back to being how it was before that child was conceived.

And if that child dies, those neural pathways don't get buried along with them. They stay there, on high alert, ready to respond to every cry, every need.

Through that week when Molly lay unconscious, her brain dead, every cell of my body was still responding to her aliveness. And that continues today.

That's why a grieving mother can never let go.

That's why a grieving mother will always keep hoping for a miracle.

Because a child should never be dead.

~

The last thing the doctors and nurses did that afternoon was to take the ventilator off Molly's mouth. They explained that they would put it back on, that Molly wouldn't be taken off life support until we were ready, until everyone had had the chance to say goodbye, but that they needed to remove it for a few minutes as a kind of test, to prove that she couldn't breathe for herself. I watched the line on one of the machines rising and rising, indicating how the carbon dioxide was going up in her body because she wasn't receiving oxygen. If someone is still alive and they're taken off the ventilator like this, there's a point at which their body would be so starved of oxygen that they would gasp for air. *Huuuuh!* They would breathe in the air. But Molly didn't.

I hated watching this procedure most of all. I begged them to put the ventilator back on so that she could breathe, but they had to wait a certain amount of time to be sure that she wouldn't gasp for air. I thought that they were killing her.

After a while, they placed the mask back on her face. The oxygen levels steadied.

"We're sorry, Molly," they said again. "We just had to show your mom and dad and your sister that your body can't wake up."

I turned a corner in that room that afternoon, watching Molly's unresponsive body. I knew she wasn't coming back. I knew from that moment I saw her legs melting into the sheets a few hours before we moved her to the children's hospital. And maybe even earlier than that. I had this gut instinct from the beginning. But I still fought it. I still kept hoping.

But Charlene had been right. Harrowing as this procedure was, watching Molly's body being poked and prodded helped carry me a few steps forward in letting go. I don't think I could have gone ahead with the unplugging if I hadn't seen with my own eyes that there was nothing we could do to wake Molly up.

The doctors, following the protocols of our state, had proved Molly was dead. Now, my heart had to believe it too.

After the procedure to certify Molly's death, we brought the visitors back in for a bit more time with Molly.

Chapter 16

Molly Facing Me

By Friday evening, the last of the visitors had left. It was hard to ask them to leave, but they understood. I did ask that if anyone showed up at the door, they not be turned away. Just one family arrived after that and their goodbye to Molly was lovely.

Gracie got in bed with Molly and just lay with her, snuggling her like they'd done a million times in our family bed and in the twin beds in their bedroom back home.

Kenny held Molly's hand.

That night, still in Molly's room, we switched on the news and saw a piece on Molly.

They interviewed the head of her dance school, Miss Cindy. She spoke about what an impact Molly made on everyone at the dance academy and how no one could get their heads around what had happened to her. She came to see Molly twice. Once, before we knew she was gone, and then once after. A stoic woman by nature, she fell to her knees that second visit and sobbed. Those who witnessed it were speechless.

There were bits of my voice in the newscast that they'd recorded over the phone. I sounded calm and confident, explaining the death of my child. For now, I was keeping the chaos of my emotions inside.

It was heart-wrenching to watch. And it made it real to

us all over again. If Molly's death was being discussed on the news, then she really wasn't going to wake up again. We sat and talked about the week. Dr. Dennis joined us for a bit. Sometimes it was silent. All of us knowing that this was the last time we would be a physical family of four.

After a while, Gracie and Kenny went back to David's House. I stayed with Molly. I had slept in the bed with her Wednesday and Thursday night. I offered the spot to Kenny and Gracie, but they declined. A part of me was relieved. She slept in the bed with me her first day on earth, she would sleep with me on her last.

As I lay beside her in the hospital bed, hearing her heart still beating under her ribcage, along with the beeping of the machines that were keeping her alive, I thought through all the hundreds of people who had come to say goodbye to Molly: people who had taught me who my little girl really was, the girl who lived and breathed out in the world beyond our front door, a girl whom—it turns out—I knew less about than I ever realized.

~

I slept better that Friday night than I had all week, lying in the bed, holding Molly, just the two of us. When I woke up, I felt calmer.

Maybe it was the sheer exhaustion of the past seven days. Or maybe it was more than that, maybe I was finally coming to terms with the fact that this was the end of the road. That today, we'd leave the hospital without our little girl. That there wasn't going to be a miracle. That she would never wake up. I was discovering that sometimes the terrible certainties bring greater calm than the constant hoping.

I woke up in the early hours of the morning, it wasn't quite light yet in the room. But it struck me straight away that something strange had happened overnight.

I rubbed my eyes. And that's when I saw it.

All week, Molly had lain motionless on her back, her eyes closed. We'd prayed for her to show us a tiny tremor of movement to indicate that her brain was still working, but her body remained still as a ghost.

But now, she was on her side turned toward me, her face right in front of mine. Which, for a few seconds, felt like the most normal and wonderful thing in the world. Until it hit me that it was impossible; she couldn't have moved by herself in the night.

Lying there, looking at her face, it all came back to me like the memories would over and over in the coming months and years, sucking me into my world that was Molly. The tiniest trigger flinging me back into the world I used to live in. The one where I still had two daughters.

That morning, the memories of Molly and Gracie when they were little and we all still slept together, the four of us in our big bed upstairs, came rushing back.

I still think it's strange that people complain so much about bedtime routines and how hard it is to get their kids to sleep. For us, it wasn't ever a discussion. The girls would get home from their activities or from school and after dinner Kenny would give them a bath.

After bath time, we'd all brush our teeth in the upstairs bathroom and get into our pj's and then tumble into bed together. Sometimes, we'd watch a Disney movie together. Gracie loved to take the disc out of the machine, put it back in its case, and switch the TV off. She was practical, always good at these kinds of processes.

Some nights, we'd play games. We'd blow up a balloon and take it upstairs and all get onto the bed and kick it up to the ceiling and see how long we could keep it in the air. Other times, we read books or just chatted. Sometimes, Kenny and I would stay awake in bed a little later than the girls to watch a show or I'd do some grading in bed. But most days, I was so exhausted from teaching and coaching and Kenny was tuckered out from driving the vending truck around all over the place, we'd all just crash together at around 8:00 p.m., our limbs all tangled up.

Kenny and I worked long hours during the week but as soon as we got home, and all night, we were there for the girls. I wouldn't change those long hours we spent with them for anything in the world. They bring me comfort now that Molly is gone.

Gracie was the soft, squishy, cuddly one. Her body just melted into ours wherever she ended up in bed. We joked about how Molly was all elbows and knees. She was skinny and tall and gangly and somehow never quite sat right. They were different that way. But it still worked. The four of us like that, curled up together.

Sometimes, if I had a late meeting at school, I'd come in and find the three of them passed out together. Molly with her legs swung over Kenny's belly. Gracie tucked into his armpit. Kenny snoring away, oblivious. I loved seeing them together like that.

Other evenings, I'd come in and the TV screen would be blue, and Gracie would be sitting on the end of the bed, her eyes wide, Kenny and Molly already asleep. I'd kiss Gracie and tell her that I was just going to brush my teeth and that I'd be in soon. By the time I came back, she'd climbed into bed and fallen asleep. Kenny told me how Gracie wanted to wait for me, no matter how long it took. I guess that somewhere in her little body, she wanted to make sure that I was home safe so that she could sleep.

Over the years, we adopted different positions in the bed.

When Gracie was a baby, before Molly was born, I'd lie her on one side, so she could nurse, and in the morning, I'd pump the other breast. She loved to sleep with us. She found it hard when Molly came along two years later and had to share her with me. I wanted to give Molly the same attention as I'd given

Gracie. They both needed so much of me.

I remember one night, how after nursing Molly, I turned to look at Gracie. Her back was turned to me, and I could hear these tiny, whimpering cries. She missed me. I was there, right next to her physically, but she felt my emotional absence as I was consumed by caring for a newborn. I pulled her in close and wrapped my arms around her and kissed her and told her that I loved her, but she kept crying. Gracie had a common phrase those days: "Molly Down, Mommy," she commanded. Often, I gave in and put Molly down and scooped Gracie up. Molly didn't mind or notice, she was too little. Gracie needed me. And I didn't want Gracie to resent her sister. I wanted them to be best friends forever.

And then, one day, Molly was in the kitchen in her high-chair laughing with Gracie dancing around her, entertaining her. They smiled at each other and were completely lost in that moment of sisterhood. Kenny and I looked at each other across the room and I whispered, "We did it! They love each other."

And from that moment, until the day Molly died, it was like they were one person: MollyGracie GracieMolly. Two halves of a whole.

~

For a long time, Molly and Gracie kept sleeping with us in the big bed.

My mom had given me an extra-long twin she didn't need anymore, and we'd added it to our bed to extend the king. Kenny slept on that. When the girls were younger, I lay at the bottom of the bed horizontally to give them more space at the top. Gracie called the spot where I slept "da bottom da bed." Sometimes, in her small, sweet voice, she'd whisper through the dark room, "Can I sleep da bottom da bed?" and I'd say yes. And then Molly would join in too and we'd all end up squished together at the bottom.

When they grew taller, I came back into the main part of the bed and slept between them.

In the mornings, just as naturally, we'd wake up together and begin our day.

I loved that our days were bookended by this togetherness. I loved the easiness of it.

For Christmas 2009, Santa finally brought the girls their own bedroom. They'd never wanted one until now, but when their friends came around to play and asked to see where they slept, they'd started feeling a bit embarrassed at not having anything to show them. On Christmas Eve, we had a neighborhood tradition of setting up a big campfire outside. While the girls played, Kenny put together the twin beds, one against the wall for Molly, one near the door for Gracie. We'd emptied the room. Painted the walls and refurbished a couple of old dressers. Later that night, while they slept, we put up wall decals and rolled out a new rug.

The girls woke up to a new bedroom.

I have a photograph of them on Christmas morning sitting on their new rug in the middle of their new bedroom, playing with a new craft.

They had their own bedroom now, but that didn't mean that was where they slept. For a long time, they kept coming back to our bed. And then, I offered to sleep in the yellow room next to theirs with the door open as a kind of transition. Often, they'd come in and sleep with me there or go back to the bed where Kenny was. They had a bedroom to show off to their friends, but they still wanted to sleep with us.

I remember the first night they slept through in their own bedroom. It was spring 2010. I'd read Harry Potter to them and tucked them in. They both put on the "blindfold masks" they loved to sleep with. And the next thing I knew, it was morning and Molly was screeching from her bedroom, "I did it! I slept all night in my bed!" She was so excited.

And that was that. By second and fourth grade they were sleeping in their own room. But they didn't always stick to their own beds. Often, I'd find Gracie in Molly's bed in the morning. They were so used to sleeping together. They kept doing it until Molly died.

It's no wonder that Gracie and I wouldn't be able to sleep upstairs for over two years after Molly's death.

~

I kissed Molly's cheek and got out of the hospital bed. Just then, Gina, Molly's night nurse, came in.

"Did you move Molly in the night?" I asked her.

She shook her head. "Move her? No."

"When I woke up this morning, she was facing me." I pointed to the bed, where Molly's head on the pillow was still facing the side where I'd slept.

"Or maybe someone else did. One of the other nurses?"

"No, they wouldn't have done that," Gina said.

My heart jolted.

"So, she moved herself?" I asked.

Gina didn't answer.

"Or I moved her in my sleep?"

Gina came to sit on the edge of the bed.

"You know that whenever you're with her, her levels settle," she explained. "I don't know how or why that's possible, only that you're her mom and that somehow having you close makes her feel better. Maybe you moved her without realizing it. Maybe your weight on the mattress shifted her over. Or maybe there's another explanation that we don't have right now. Things happen that we can't always find reasons for." She smiled.

This is why I loved the nurses here. They understood that there was so much more to what was happening to Molly than any of us could explain or understand.

And my heart wanted to believe that there was another explanation, too, in the way we cling to meaning and hope in the most meaningless of times.

When a tragedy like this happens, when you lose a child, your understanding of how the universe works gets bigger and wider and deeper than ever before. All the rational explanations remain, but you know that there's more to this world and more beyond this world too. That most times, the explanations don't cancel each other out. Molly's body might have shifted under my weight, but that didn't mean that she didn't also choose to face me as we slept together too.

Molly would have known how much it meant to me to wake up looking into her beautiful face, her soft skin, as though she were back home in our bed like when she and Gracie were little and we all slept together.

She knows everything now, I think. Before, when she was alive, she had to guess at it. She had to ask questions. Her acts of kindness were leaps of faith. But from where she is now, she knows completely. She can read my heart. And there's some comfort in that.

This *knowing* I believe Molly now has, wherever she is, reminds me of something she said when her grandfather, Papa Gordy, Kenny's dad, died. She was only eight years old when I told her and Gracie that he was gone. Their responses were classic.

Gracie had a rose-tinted vision of the world. When we flushed a spider down the toilet, she smiled, thinking about how the spider was going off to play with her friends at the sewage treatment plant. For her, Papa Gordy was in heaven now. He was happy. We would miss him but for him, all was well.

Molly sat straight up.

"Wait, you mean he knows everything now?" she said, wide-eyed.

We looked at her, puzzled by her excitement.

"What do you mean, Molly?" I asked.

"If he's dead and he's in heaven, it means he knows every-thing, he has all the answers, he gets it all."

So, that's what Molly thought death was. A final solution to the riddle of life. My clever, intellectual little girl.

"Yes, he has all the answers now," I said.

"Wow," she said, shaking her head in disbelief. "He's so lucky."

That hit me hard. How her little mind saw death as a good thing because it meant you had the answers.

Well, now you have all the answers, Molly, I thought, look-ing at her body lying there on the hospital bed a few hours away from being unplugged.

I turned to Sharon, another nurse who cared for Molly.

"I thought it was your day off," I said.

"It was. But I asked to be here."

Molly was Sharon's first patient here. She'd just started working at the hospital; the job was so new that she was still living in a hotel room out of a suitcase. I sometimes feel like she came to work here just for us. Because we needed some-one just like her with her shock of red hair and her kind smile and her way of understanding what was going on beyond the medical procedures. Although Molly arrived at the children's hospital unconscious and never once woke up, I could tell that she and Sharon had a special connection. Sharon spoke to Mol-ly as though she knew her. As though she were still alive. As though she might still wake up.

And Sharon was there for Gracie too. Every time we were called into a meeting or had to deal with something concern-ing Molly's care or were busy with visitors, Sharon would sit with Gracie, sometimes for hours, just holding her or listening to her or letting her cry on her shoulder.

Today was her day off, but she came in for Molly. For us.

When Sharon was done checking on Molly, I went off to get myself a coffee. I walked around the hospital in a daze, trying not to think about what was going to happen in a few hours, that Molly would be unplugged from all those machines and that we'd go home without her.

Kenny had an early morning dialysis session organized by our social worker, so it would take him a while to get to us. Watching him, I thought again about how he was the one I thought would die first. Before any of us. I could never have imagined that the person I'd lose would be Molly. Sweet, vibrant, full-of-life, thirteen-year-old Molly.

But death doesn't work to our human logic. For now, it had left Kenny alone and it had taken Molly.

Gracie had to wait for a ride from David's House because the walk to Molly's ward was too far.

So, I still had some time with Molly. In a few hours, I'd be leaving the hospital without her. I needed every second I had left with her.

Chapter 17

Footprints

When Kenny and Gracie arrived, our social worker took us aside and said that she wanted to do something with us, something important, something that would help us process Molly's death.

She was a kind woman with long hair and glasses. She'd been with us since Tuesday night when we learned that Molly wasn't going to wake up. She and her team took care of everything. Kenny's dialysis. Our medications. Kenny and Gracie's stay at David's House. The social worker who'd set up grief groups and classes and monthly mailings for years to come. I wasn't in a place to recognize it then, but I can say it now: the work these social workers do is phenomenal.

"We think it's important for you to have some memories of Molly as part of saying goodbye," she said.

My stomach churned. I had all the memories I needed of Molly. What could she possibly mean?

"We've found that certain things can help with grieving families," she explained. "One of those is to take footprints and handprints of both you and Molly. And fingerprints too. You can take them home."

I didn't want to take home handprints and fingerprints. I wanted to take Molly home.

"We've found that the process is important too," she went

on. "That it's a healing moment for families."

I'm not sure now why I reacted so badly to her suggestions. They were kind and thoughtful, but it somehow felt like a stupid thing to do. Something contrived by a bunch of social workers who could never understand what it felt like to lose a child. These social workers had worked with hundreds of families who'd lost loved ones. They knew what they were doing. But still, I didn't like what I was being asked to do.

Maybe it was because there was a voice in my head too, saying: *Isn't this the kind of thing you do to mark the beginning of life—taking a baby's footprints as a souvenir for when they're all grown up and wearing huge sneakers? Isn't this what you do before you take your baby home and start the rest of their lives?*

Only, Molly wasn't at the beginning of her life; she was at the end of it. And I wasn't in the maternity ward, I was in the PICU, the place where kids come to die.

And I felt that doing this was making a statement about our family that I wasn't yet ready to accept.

We weren't welcoming our newest member, a baby.

We weren't celebrating Molly joining and expanding the lives that up until now we'd lived, just the four of us.

We were saying goodbye. Our family was shrinking. It felt all wrong.

"Why are we doing this?" I asked again.

"It will help," the social worker said. "You don't have to do this, but I think it would be a good thing."

Her voice sounded firm, like somehow, even though she was giving us an option, she was making it clear that this is what we should do. I was too tired to fight it and I liked her, she'd been kind. So, I went along with it.

On the shelf at the end of Molly's bed, she set up the paints: green for Kenny, blue for me, purple for Gracie, and, naturally, pink for Molly.

And then, we took turns to paint Molly's feet.

Gracie, Kenny, and I passed the brush of pink paint between us and ran it along the soles of Molly's long, delicate feet. In the end, I think this was the most healing part of it. Not having the footprints—though I value them now—but touching Molly. Connecting with her body, a body I had conceived and carried for nine months and birthed and cared for, for thirteen years. A body I loved. So much of hospital life seems clinical and designed to keep patients' bodies at a distance, the machines and the bed rails and all the paraphernalia of sickness and death. In this moment, as we painted her feet and pressed them to the 9-by-9-inch white canvas that the social worker had given us, I felt closer to Molly than I'd felt all week. Her soft, translucent skin in the palms of my hands, the weight of her ankles.

I realize, too, that it was one of the few times that week when it was just the three of us with Molly. There were so many visitors. So many teams of doctors and nurses. Everyone rushing in and out all the time. Everyone claiming a bit of Molly. For that hour, as we held Molly's hands and feet and fingers and as we painted our own, it felt like we'd gone home and were sitting again, just the four of us, around the kitchen table or on the brown sofa in the living room. That we were a family.

And there was something about washing her hands and her feet too. It reminded me of a sacrament, of a cleansing.

On Wednesday, we'd washed Molly's body to prepare her for visitors. A week later, before her funeral, I'd wash her with rosewater again as is customary in the Bahá'í faith. But this was different somehow. This small, colorful, intimate moment with Molly. She loved doing crafts. If she'd been alive, she'd have found this fun.

After washing her feet, we did our handprints together, each in our favorite colors. So now we have a canvas with all our hands. Our family, as it was meant to be, four sets of handprints rather than the three that now remain.

The last thing we did was to take Molly's fingerprints. We

put them on a piece of paper; they're in my filing cabinet. I've been meaning for a while to have a necklace made with Molly's handprints. Or maybe, if Kenny and I chose to get married again, to have them on our rings. Gracie said she'd love us to make something special, to have our fingerprints alongside hers in a tangible form. Maybe one of these days, I'll get around to doing something with them.

The canvases sat for nearly two years in a room off our living room where all the things from Molly's stay at the hospital got dumped when we went home. For a long time, I couldn't bring myself to touch them or look at them or think about them. Now, we've brought the canvases out. They're on the stairs along with the dance costumes that Molly never again got to wear.

Our social worker was right. When I look back at it, I'm utterly grateful. Although I didn't want to do it at the time and although I couldn't look at those canvases for years, I'm glad we have them now. I'm glad she forced me a little to do something that I didn't understand then.

I'm grateful now for anything at all we have left of Molly.

Chapter 18

A Dimmer,
Not a Toggle Switch

People who haven't experienced death up close might be mistaken in thinking that it's an absolute thing, that there's a clear line between when there's life and when it ends. In most cases, the process is messier than that, grayer and more gradual and much slower than you expect.

Looking back at that week and at this moment when we had to unplug Molly, I'm struck by how long the process took.

At just about lunchtime, Kenny, Gracie, and I got ready to say goodbye.

There was a whole team in the room during the procedure that would take my little girl off life support.

Chaz was there, "Nurse Charlie," with whom I'd shared two important years when we were still young and carefree and childless.

Sharon was there to help on her day off.

There was another day nurse on that I didn't know.

The social worker who'd been with us all week.

Then there was Dennis, the doctor who was overall in charge of Molly's case that week.

My brother, Jonathan, came with his wife, Lan Lan, whom I asked to take pictures.

People found it strange how I wanted to document it all. I teased Chaz, telling him to smile.

"I can't," he said, his lips tight.

"She's been set free, Chaz, it's OK to smile," I said.

He still couldn't do it.

He didn't get it. Why would you want to take snapshots of your daughter's death? But I was the kind of mom who documented everything. Every dance recital, every birthday and Christmas, every funny pose that Molly and Gracie struck to entertain me, every outfit they put on for Halloween. This moment, too, was part of Molly's story. I wanted to have memories of her right until the end.

Caity, Kenny's daughter from his first marriage, was there too.

My mother wasn't there. She and my sister-in-law, Cathy, wanted to be with Ricky, my brother, while Molly was unplugged. He was experiencing his own sort of loss and couldn't be there. At a time in his life when he should have been slowing down and enjoying the outcome of years of hard work, my brother found himself faced with a tragedy as painful as mine. The thing is, while Ricky was going through this, he did some amazing things. He spent time in meaningful reflection. He looked at himself and at those around him and called out the good in what he saw. He was helpful, smart and kind, like Molly.

Recently, he came for Thanksgiving, and I told him how I was still trying to get my head around why I was the one who had to lose a child. What my lesson or purpose was. Some people say that every mother is chosen for her specific child, no matter how that mother or child's life turns out. I still think about that all the time: What I can do with what happened to Molly. This book is part of me working that out. After listening to me for a while, Ricky said, "It's like me and what I've been through. I was meant to experience that." Considering everything Ricky's been through, that felt like an incredible statement. I wish that he and Molly had spent more time together as she grew up. She would have liked him. His spirit. His honesty. And how they both saw a purpose even in the hardest of situations.

When we could finally reunite, the first thing we did was meet at Molly's grave. She had been gone a while now. Cathy, Kenny and Gracie joined us for a bittersweet welcome to Molly's new home. I would have loved Ricky and Molly to get to know each other better. Had they been able to spend more time together, he could have helped her understand the complex ways the world can mistreat people and how you can do good things with your life, regardless of what it throws at you.

The unplugging procedure took longer than any of us were prepared for. We all took turns to hold Molly's hand and kiss her and stroke her arm. Gracie had a hard time. She broke down and Sharon held her and talked to her.

There's so much more keeping a body alive than just a breathing machine. When you watch the procedure on TV, they just pull a plug and it's over. In real life, it's not like that at all. It takes a long time. And there's a lot to do to switch off a life. And I believe now—I guess I've always believed it, but Molly's death really brought it home to me—the transition between life isn't a toggle switch, an on/off button, but a dimmer switch. And, more than this, I have a suspicion that it never really goes off altogether. There's a reason we feel the spirit of those who have passed around us.

The amount of fluid, hormones, and chemicals that it takes to keep a body alive on life support is huge. It's not just making the lungs breathe. That's part of it, but when life is over and the brain is no longer talking to the body, the doctors must work hard to keep the body viably healthy.

Molly had three IVs in her arms and four bags.

The first thing they did was to switch off all the monitors. They did this for us so that we wouldn't have to hear the beeping or watch those jagged lines as the life went out of Molly.

There were so many screens: screens to monitor her heart rate, her carbon dioxide levels, her blood pressure. All of that had to be disconnected.

Once the screens went blank, the room felt quieter and darker.

Then, very slowly, they began to pull all the needles out and, as they did, they wiped down her skin.

My overriding memory of this process was how kind they were, especially Chaz. He and his team were careful and meticulous in everything they did. Professional and kind. The opposite of what we'd experienced at home. And he never stopped talking to Molly. The irony was that as he was taking away the apparatus that would ensure her death, he talked to her like she was still alive. "I'm sorry if this is hurting you, Molly," he said and, "You're doing a great job." The respect he showed my little girl's body—and us, as her family—was profound.

Twenty-six years earlier, on Halloween, when Chaz and I were going out, we'd hiked to the top of a mountain and made love under a full moon. And here he was, nearly three decades later, unplugging my child and helping me through his kindness and tenderness to say goodbye. I was reminded, again, of how miracles show up even in our darkest hours. Perhaps they show up brightest of all *because* of the darkness. I was so grateful that it was him, someone I knew and loved, who'd shared those important years with me, who was here, doing this.

From pulling the first plug and IV to the final beat of her heart was about an hour. A long, slow process that allowed us, too, to get our heads and our hearts around what was happening.

The final piece was taking away all the apparatus on Molly's face. Her breathing tube and mask, the bits that covered up her mouth and her cheeks. I realized that I hadn't seen my child's face, not properly, not fully, since Sunday.

When it was all done, Chaz said, "If you want, you can climb into bed with her now, Barb."

So, I got in with her and held her tight. She still felt so warm and alive.

Everyone else kept milling around.

And we waited for Molly's heart to stop. It struck me how it didn't just stop right away. How it kept beating for a good fifteen minutes after all the IVs and machines and tubes and breathing mechanisms had been taken away.

The heart is its own entity, I remember thinking. It beats to its own time. It doesn't just stop. That felt miraculous somehow.

Every few minutes, the overseeing doctor would put his head around the door and say, "Forty-two bpm now ..."

Then, "Thirty-one beats now ..."

A few minutes later he'd say, "Twelve bpm..." He was watching a monitor outside the room.

I lay next to her with my hand on her chest and the thought that came rushing to me at that moment was how I'd been the first to hear Molly's heart when she was a baby living inside me. All those doctor appointments when they'd put the monitor on my belly, and I'd hear that galloping heartbeat coming from my womb. That I was the first one to feel her move too. And here I was, lying with her on her deathbed, listening to and feeling her heart stopping.

I stretched out my arm to Kenny.

"Come and feel this," I said, like I'd said when he came with me to those prenatal appointments or when I felt her kick.

He walked over to her bed and put his hand on Molly's heart and felt it slow.

Then Dennis put his head around the door one last time.

"OK, she's gone," he said.

And then it stopped, and I couldn't feel anything anymore.

I'll never forget feeling those last beats of Molly's heart and what that felt like and how it changed me forever.

A heart that had lived inside me for nine months and then lived out in the world as she grew, pulsing through her every moment as she danced and sang and studied and lived and loved and walked and slept.

One moment it was here.

And then, at noon exactly, on the seventh of May 2016, it was gone.

Today, I'm still trying to make sense of the time between that last beat and the time in which I live now, a space I'll spend the rest of my life trying to navigate. Because, in truth, I keep expecting there to be another beat after that last one. That's how the heart works. Especially the hearts of our children. They're meant to beat on and on long past our own.

Slowly, the doctors and nurses and social worker left the room.

I lay beside Molly for over two hours.

I vaguely heard movements around the bed as Kenny and other members of our family cleaned up, putting things into plastic bags, packing things up, taking things off the walls. They carried out all the things that had accumulated through the week to our cars. Gifts and clothes and posters and photographs and memories. Nurse Sharon took care of Gracie. I couldn't at that moment. I had to be with Molly, just the two of us, like we were at the beginning of her life.

I told her, over and over, that I loved her. I held her. And I sang to her.

Everything was a song with Molly.

I remember one song we shared when she was little. Molly had a hard time with transitions, with letting go of one stage of life for another. For a long time, I couldn't get her out of Pull-Ups. She associated them with a time in her life when she was happy. Whenever I suggested we use the potty and get rid of them, she cried and cried. So, I didn't push it. When people raised their eyebrows or made comments, I'd say, "It's not my butt. She's the one who must sit in her poop." I believed in trusting children and their instincts.

Kenny had a phrase, a mix of pee and poop and/or tinkling

that came out as Stinky PooTinky. Whenever Molly needed to have her diaper changed, I'd sing: "Stinky PooTinky ... Stinky PooTinky ..." And it would make her smile. I remember once bringing her to the bathroom just off the kitchen and changing her on the floor. I sang softly to her as I cleaned her up and then I noticed this tiny, tiny little voice joining in, "Stinky PooTinky ..." Her big eyes looked up at me as she sang.

So, I sang it to her, to my little girl whose heartbeat had gone but who was still there on the hospital bed in my arms. "Stinky PooTinky ..." I sang. Because it somehow brought back the best of our times together.

In those moments after Molly's death, I apologized to her for all the mistakes I'd made. For not being there the last week of her life. I promised her that I'd never let anyone forget the extraordinary person that she was and the beautiful thirteen years she'd had in the world. And that I wouldn't let the story of what happened to her go unheard. That I'd fight for the rights of young women to be heard and seen and given the treatment they deserved.

And then, again, I told her, over and over, that I loved her.

As I spoke to her, I took a cloth and washed her arms and her legs and her face. Her beautiful, flawless skin. I still couldn't believe that she was gone.

Still, now, I feel that rush of disbelief that it's possible to have a child and for her to be gone.

~

When the room was empty and it was time to go, I started to panic. I couldn't get off the bed.

I'd been prepared for every stage of this week—but not this. Not the end. Not the leaving.

"What happens now?" I asked Chaz. My voice choked.

Before he even answered, I got a picture of it. We would leave the room and drive home and Molly would stay here alone. And then, her naked thirteen-year-old body would be taken down to the morgue by some orderly.

No. No. I couldn't let that happen. I couldn't let a stranger take my daughter and put her in a refrigerated box.

"Please, Chaz, please. I don't want Molly to be alone. I'll take her down myself. I'll stay with her -"

He touched my arm gently.

"I'll do it," he said. "I'll take her down and look after her and stay with her until she's safely locked in the drawer. I'll make sure she's OK.

The mechanics of death are horrible. The machines. The operations. The terminology like unplugging. The notion of your little girl being in a refrigerated drawer. I wished for something softer and kinder, something more human than all of this.

Just when I thought I'd done all the hard things already, another one reared up in front of me. Saying goodbye one last time, knowing that when I saw her next, she would look very different. That without life support, her body was going to change. That out of this hospital room there was no longer any chance of her waking up. I couldn't imagine myself walking out of that room, leaving Molly behind, and never coming back. Being in that hospital room with Molly that week had become my routine, my life. I didn't know how to function any other way. Living in a world without Molly felt as impossible as breathing without oxygen. She was my life. And now I had to live without her.

But I didn't have a choice, did I?

I had to leave the child I'd conceived and grown in my womb for nine months.

I had to leave her here, amongst strangers, and go home to a place where she should be but never would be again.

Leaving the hospital that day, without Molly, was the hardest thing I've ever done.

Part II:

AFTER SHE'D GONE

Chapter 19

The Maple
and the Dragonfly

We filled our car with all the stuff from Molly's hospital room, a whole lifetime of balloons and cards and posters and gifts in just five days, and got in.

Gracie sat in the front with Kenny, and I sat in the back. We stopped by David's House to collect their things. And then, we turned onto I-89 and headed home. Without Molly.

It was a cold, rainy, crappy day. As I watched the rain hitting the windshield, I kept asking myself what we would be doing today if Molly hadn't died, if all this hadn't happened. I'd have been home from Amsterdam for a week now. We'd have gotten back into our routines. Molly would probably be giving me a hard time about having gone off with Roy, but she'd be OK. She'd be happy and planning her future. She'd be alive.

Much of the drive was a blur. I'd come to learn that this would become a pattern in how my mind worked, how one moment I'd be thinking intensely about Molly and how she should still be alive and what she'd be doing and then I'd panic, realizing she was dead. I remember the words ricocheting in my mind: dead Molly, dead Molly, dead Molly. And then my brain would sink into a fog, and I'd make my way through hours and days without even noticing them passing. I suppose it's the brain's way of coping with trauma.

There's another panic that set in during the drive home, one that recurred again and again in the following months, often in the middle of the night: my fear that Molly had disappeared—even her dead body was gone—and I couldn't find her.

For thirteen years, she'd been my living child and even this last week in the hospital, I'd been there next to her body. And now, it felt like she was nowhere. I didn't understand how such a thing was possible.

When we were nearly home, Chaz called me to say that Molly was safe. He'd taken her to the morgue, and they'd locked her drawer and he was going to check on her again soon. It seems impossible that I could be grateful at a time like this, grateful when my daughter was lying in a hospital morgue. But I was grateful for Chaz. At least Molly had someone I knew and loved looking after her. The impersonal nature of the processes and systems that surround death deepen the pain and the trauma. I was lucky that I had him.

When we got home, my friend Robyn was there with her daughters, Maddie and Jordan. She'd asked people to bring pink and purple flowers, Molly's and Gracie's favorite colors. Some of those plants are still alive today in the garden in the front yard. On this gray, cold, rainy day, our yard was a sea of color. It reminded me of Molly, of how she was in the world.

We emptied the car and put everything into the small room off the living room. All those things that people had brought for Molly: clothes and flowers and plushies and food and other gifts. We wouldn't touch that room for another two years.

There were tons of food. Kenny brought some of it into the kitchen and said he'd prepare something for us later. Then he turned to me and said, "I'm going to the liquor store." His voice was tired.

Alcohol has always been part of our routine as a couple. A way to numb the harsher edges of life. When he got into financial trouble with his business. When I lost my job as a teacher.

When our relationship fell apart. If there was a time when we needed something to numb us, it was now.

"Sure," I said. I understood why he needed it. We both did.

Looking back at the months and years that followed I realize how naïve that assumption was, that a little alcohol to numb the emotions was a good idea. That it was normal. Sure, it's normalized by our society. It's a way of life. But using drugs to get away from the pain never ends well, and alcohol is often a slippery slope into something else. We'd both have our reckonings with that as we lived through those dark months of grief following Molly's death.

All day people came in and out.

Little A, a girl I coached at our high school, ran up to me and said that she and Robyn's daughter, Jordan, were going to have "Molly" tattoos done in town. A heart with an *M*. I watched them go off together and then Little A's mother, Janine, took me aside and said she wanted to share something.

She pointed at the big maple tree in our yard. "Molly's here," she said. "Sitting in that swing, watching us."

Over the years since Molly's death, I've come to see how people who've experienced great trauma in their lives are somehow more spiritually connected. Janine's best friend was killed by her husband; Janine adopted her friend's children. We are surrounded by so many tragedies that only seem to come to light when we've experienced one of our own. It's like a door opens, and suddenly you see all the pain and loss and trauma in the world that sometimes stays out of sight when you're a normal person going about your daily life. It's almost as though there are two worlds that exist side by side, and it takes a tragedy for you to realize that the one you're living in is only half of the truth of what it means to live on this earth.

I didn't know what to make of Janine's comment about Molly on the swing but, over the years, I've found comfort from words passed on to me from friends and strangers and psychics, those who come to me in a spirit of truth rather than wanting something in return, who have given me insights into how they see Molly now. Spiritually speaking, I'm an open kind of person. The Bahá'í Faith believes progressive revelation and so embrace many ways of seeing our world and other worlds too. There are all kinds of prophets who have spoken truths to us through time and space. Why not these people, I tell myself. And there are fleeting moments when I've seen Molly for myself. One of the moments I remember most came two years later in this same front yard with that same maple looking over us.

~

It was a hot day in August two years after Molly died. I'd booked tickets for Gracie and her friend Mykaila to see a Taylor Swift concert, and they wanted to dress up as angels, so I said I would take them to the mall in Manchester.

Gracie was born in 2001. Mykaila in 2002. Molly in 2003. The three of them had been inseparable. Molly's death had a huge effect on Mykaila. I wanted this concert to be special for her and Gracie.

Molly had loved Taylor Swift too. I'd taken the girls to her concerts twice and planned to take them to many more. One of the many bits of unfinished business that followed Molly's death. Molly would have loved to be there that day with Gracie and Mykaila, getting ready, planning what they were going to wear, giddy with excitement.

I waited for the girls in the yard. I still had the old brown Honda I had when Molly was alive. And that's when I noticed them. I felt the vibration of their wings, caught the movement of their bodies out of the corner of my eye before I saw them: two, huge, red dragonflies hovering around me and the car.

I'd never seen a red dragonfly before. The size of the insects impressed me. Their huge propeller wings. The way they swept up through the air.

One of the dragonflies stayed close to me. It hovered around the car. And then, as I moved around the yard, it followed me.

I could hear the girls coming down the steps through the house, laughing and talking. I didn't want to leave. There was something in that moment with the dragonfly that made my body fill with light in a way that I hadn't felt since before Molly's death. I just wanted to stay with it for as long as it was willing to stay with me.

The girls came down the porch steps.

"Wow!" Gracie said, stopping to look at the dragonfly.

Gracie wasn't one to notice things like that, not then. Over the years she's grown more sensitive to these sacred moments, but at seventeen, she was still wrapped up with the immediate life that stood in front of her: friends and boyfriends and clothes and shopping and Taylor Swift concerts. They were what she needed to get through losing Molly.

But still, that day she saw the dragonfly.

"Yeah, it hasn't stopped following me around," I said.

But then, as the girls walked toward me, the dragonfly joined its mate, and they flew off together. For a moment, we stood there, stunned, looking at the sky, and then we snapped back into everyday life, into driving to the mall.

To get in the mood for the concert, we listened to Taylor Swift songs in the car on the way to Manchester. For months after Molly's death, I couldn't bear to listen to music. Anything that went deep, that touched the raw places inside me, was out of bounds and music was one of those painful triggers. But over the years, I've tried, for Gracie, to allow music back into our lives. I know that she needs it. Music helps young people navigate their way through life.

For me, listening to music brought up feelings about Molly that were unbearably painful. For Gracie, listening to Taylor Swift was comforting, it made her feel close to Molly again.

In this, and in so many other ways, I've learned how personal grief is. And how to respect Gracie in her own journey.

After I'd dropped the girls off at the mall, I went to visit my friend Deb, who lived in Manchester. She'd invited me over to hang out at the pool with her while the girls shopped. It was a hot day, and I was grateful for her company. The pool belonged to her apartment complex, so one of her neighbors was there too.

I got into my swimsuit and put my towel out on the deck chair and then I felt it again. That vibration in the air. A flash of diaphanous red.

I spun round and there it was, this time on its own. The dragonfly.

"I've never seen one of those before in my whole life before today," Deb's neighbor said.

She too was struck by its size, by the majesty of its movements, by how it seemed to own the air it swam in.

My breath caught in my throat. I swallowed hard.

"How long has it been here?" I asked Deb's friend.

"Oh, it showed up right when you pulled into the parking lot," she said.

Like I said, I've always been open to the many spiritual iterations of life. My own faith is Bahá'í, taught to me by my parents. It's the form of the divine that is best suited to who I am and how I move through the world. It makes sense to me. But I know that there are as many ways of seeing God as there are people on the earth. Everything, in the end, is spiritual.

Some of my psychic friends would have leaped straight onto the dragonfly experience and given it a deep, spiritual significance.

Many people, I'm sure, would have simply enjoyed the physicality of the insect and found a perfectly plausible reason for its presence near a body of water. We had the pool up in the yard back home. There was a pool here too. The fact that I'd never seen a red dragonfly before and that I had two sightings in the space of a couple of hours was mere coincidence.

Who knows which version is right? I can only go by what

I felt that day.

The feeling that Molly was there in the red dragonfly. And that the one that was following me around the yard was the same one who showed up seventeen miles away in Manchester.

I got into the pool and the dragonfly followed me across the water. It landed on my head, its wings caught up in my curly hair. And then, when I went under the water, it went to sit on the side of the pool. As soon as I came up again, it flew back toward me.

It wouldn't leave me alone.

I told my friend Deb about the dragonflies in our yard. She smiled.

"It has to be Molly," she said, as she watched the dragonfly beating its wings around my head.

Since Molly's death, I've tried just about everything to find some peace with what happened. I've taken medication. Recreational drugs. I've gotten drunk too many times to count. I've sought spiritual guidance. Counseling. Psychotherapy. Weightlifting. I've prayed and screamed and wished I was dead and then clawed my way back to life again. A few times, I went to see psychics recommended by friends. They always said the same thing, "Molly wants you to know that it's OK, that she's happy and that it wasn't your fault. She'll find ways to come to you, to be with you, to help you feel that she loves you."

Maybe they were just telling me what I needed to hear. Maybe that's the kind of thing they say to every grieving mother who experiences guilt about her child's death and who feels like she can't go on any longer knowing that the person she brought into the world is dead. But there have been signs. Things that others have noticed, things that my heart has noticed, that have brought Molly close.

For those of us who haven't had much contact with death, life and death are such stark opposites. Life either is or isn't. Since Molly's death, I've come to see the veil between life and death as more fluid than that. I believe that the dead are with us. I wish I could bury my nose in Molly's long, sweet-smelling hair. I wish I could kiss the dimples on her shoulders. I wish I could see her huge smile and her big, soulful eyes and watch her skipping across the yard. Those physical pleasures are no longer mine to be had, but that doesn't mean that she's not here anymore. In fact, sometimes when I'm lucky, I feel as though she's closer than she ever was in the flesh because our bodies no longer separate us; she's just here, in her very purest form.

Like I believe she was on the day when those red dragonflies came to visit.

~

On the day we came back from the hospital after my friend made the comment about seeing Molly in the maple tree, I looked around the yard.

It made sense for her to hang around here, the place she'd loved so much. The trees and fence around which she'd hung fairy lights at Christmas. The patch of ground on which we put the pool each summer which attracted hundreds of friends to come and hang out with us and the girls. The driveway she and Gracie had run up and down together a million times on their way to and from school. The enchanted forest we'd made between our house and the neighbor's yard. This was where Molly lived. So, this is where her spirit would return.

Chapter 20
Molly's Eyes

The call came without warning, late on Saturday afternoon. People still filled our yard and our house. I had to go upstairs so I could hear the person on the other end of the line. I held my breath as I walked past Molly and Gracie's bedroom and the bathroom where Molly had spent her last night, lying on the floor, throwing up.

"Yes?" I said.

A woman introduced herself as working for New England Donor Services in Waltham, Massachusetts. She spoke for a while. I could hear the buzz of voices from outside and down-stairs. I was finding it hard to concentrate on what she was saying.

"We're phoning to discuss Molly's eyes—"

My mind snapped back into focus. "Oh!"

Her eyes. They wanted my sweet Molly's eyes.

I sat down on the bed. My chest heaved. I couldn't breathe.

All babies have huge eyes. It's designed to make them evolutionarily attractive so that we take extra good care of them. Scientists explain that seeing these big baby eyes trigger responses in a part of our brains involved in rewarding and decision-making. A cute baby with huge, shiny eyes is almost impossible to ignore. It's about survival.

I always remember the first time I held Molly, how huge

her eyes were—even bigger than other babies'—how she stared up at me with a thousand feelings and questions about this world she'd just been born into.

The thing is that Molly's eyes stayed that way, even when the rest of her body grew. Huge and beautiful and soulful and full of unanswered questions.

Her eyes were the first thing that people noticed about her and commented on.

And they revealed everything.

If she was angry, you knew about it through her eyes.

If she was happy, you'd see it in those dancing, sparkling eyes.

If she was wonderstruck, she didn't have to say a word, you just knew by looking at those huge eyes, wider than ever, that she'd taken in something that had moved her.

Everything had been taken from me, and now they wanted this too? To take Molly's big, beautiful, soulful eyes? It felt like yet another blow.

And yet the thought that some other person, somewhere, a child perhaps, might get to have them, wasn't that the best news too? That someone who needed to would get to see through those big, beautiful eyes. That rather than being buried with her in a casket, Molly's eyes would make that person's life better; that was a good thing. Most of all, I know that Molly would have wanted it.

So much of this process of losing Molly, of the details around her death and burial and my grief, is this constant tug-of-war between horror and beauty, between loss and life.

I took a deep breath.

"Yes," I said. "You can have her eyes."

"OK, so we'll send a team up to get her—"

My heart jolted.

"What do you mean, to *get* her?"

"Some of my colleagues will pick up her body and bring it here and we'll remove her eyes so that they can be stored safely and then used to help someone—"

"No, no, no, no, no, no."

My heart rate shot up. I started to panic.

"Ms. Higgins?"

"I'm not having strangers driving Molly around, taking her to a place I don't know. If necessary, I'll drive her myself, but I'm not letting you take her anywhere."

When I think of Molly now, buried in the ground of the cemetery a mile from my house, I know that it's just her body. That her spirit is elsewhere. The passing of time has allowed me to make that distinction. But that day, a few hours after we'd unplugged her, it was still too early for me to disconnect my Molly from her sweet, soft body—from her beautiful eyes. I couldn't bear the thought of her being alone with strangers or carted up and down a highway in a truck.

"I want you to have her eyes," I explained, trying to sound calm. "But you must understand. She's my child. I can't let you have her like this. I just can't stand the thought of it."

"I understand," she said, her voice kind. "Leave it with me. I'll get back to you."

In the years that followed Molly's death, I did some research and came to understand that there's a huge shortage of corneas available for transplantation, not only in the US but around the world. The need far exceeds the availability. So, this woman in Waltham wasn't going to give up easily; she needed Molly's eyes.

Half an hour or so later she called back.

"I understand your concerns," she said. "I have a daughter."

So much of my relationship to others in the years following Molly's death would be determined by people like her, those who were able to reach me on a human level because they could empathize with having a child. Even if they had never lost a child, just having one combined with the power a mother always has to imagine the horror of losing the thing she loves most, that's enough for there to be a connection. For me to feel seen and heard. A mother understands why, when you've just lost a child, there are just some things you can't allow. At this moment, I couldn't bear for Molly's dead body to be carted around.

"It's unconventional, but we've arranged for our team to go to the hospital to remove Molly's eyes there," the woman explained. "Then they'll bring them back to our facility here in Waltham. I promise we won't move her. We've contacted the hospital, and they've agreed to help us." She paused. "Is that OK with you, Ms. Higgins?"

I breathed out. "Thank you."

When I hung up, I called Chaz right away; I knew he was still working his shift.

He promised me that he'd be there with Molly when they came for her eyes.

I found out later from the hospital that because of my request for Molly that day, they've changed the protocol when it comes to children. Organ donor facilities come to the hospital to take the organs rather than transporting them unnecessarily and adding to the strain and trauma on families. It was a way in which Molly's story has helped grieving families. My hope is that it will be the first of many, many ways in which Molly's life—and death—improves the lives of the most vulnerable in our society. That the treatment of children—and girls in particular—will become better because of what Molly went through.

Chapter 21

The First Night

It was dark by the time the last of the visitors left that Saturday night.

The house was a mess. Piles of food still littered the back porch. Gracie, Kenny, and I were exhausted. All I wanted was to go to sleep. But then it hit me: this was our first night back in our home without Molly. And I began to panic again like I would over a million things big and small that reminded me that Molly was never coming back and that somehow I had to get through life without her. It didn't seem possible.

I looked at Gracie, standing in the living room, and knew that she felt as overwhelmed as I did. How could she go back and sleep in the room that she and Molly had shared?

We all felt it, that home would never be the same again.

Kenny poured himself a drink and went up to the bedroom. Perhaps men find it easier. Or perhaps his dialysis-dependent body ached so much that he knew he needed a proper bed.

Gracie and I grabbed some pillows and blankets from the couch and threw them down on the living room floor. Neither of us could face going upstairs; there was too much of Molly there. And that was a new kind of closeness. A togetherness in our grief. There were many times in the coming weeks and months and years when we'd feel lost to each other, unable to understand each other's particular grief. But there were times, too, like this, when we came together knowing that only we understood each other's worlds now.

And there was another dimension to this sleeping downstairs, camping on the living room floor. As we lay curled up, holding each other, I think we both kidded ourselves that if we slept here, if we did something out of the ordinary, something that felt temporary and makeshift, then maybe tomorrow, we'd wake up and carry our pillows and blankets back upstairs, straighten up the living room, and Molly would come running through the door. That maybe tomorrow, everything would go back to normal.

What we didn't know was that there was no normal to go back to. That it would be another year and a half before Gracie finally moved back upstairs. Another four years before she'd find the strength to start tidying up the things Molly had left behind on her side of the room: her phone still plugged into the socket next to her bedside table, candy left over from Easter stuffed into her drawers, the things they'd bought at the mall the week before she died in a plastic bag with the receipt.

As for me, it would take me even longer than Gracie to get up off that living room floor.

At midnight, Chaz called me to say that the funeral home had come to collect Molly from the hospital, that she was on her way home.

Chapter 22
Mother's Day

As soon as I woke up on Sunday morning, the first day home without Molly, I suddenly remembered what day it was. Had the weight on my chest not felt so unbearably heavy, I would have laughed at the irony of it. Of all the Sundays in the year, *this* Sunday, the day after we unplugged Molly, was Mother's Day.

I looked over at Gracie curled up in a ball between a bunch of couch cushions and blankets. She was still asleep. I prayed that she would sleep for hours, that she'd be kept for as long as possible from this day which she should have been sharing with Molly. For years I'd find myself having to do this doublethink, processing what a particular situation without Molly would mean for me and what it would mean for Gracie. I was the mother of a dead child having to go through Mother's Day. Gracie would have to go through Mother's Day without her sister. She would have to face it for the first time in her memory as an only child.

And what made it worse was that we both knew that Molly would have been up hours ago, excitedly planning things as she did for every special day of the year.

Molly loved celebrating holidays. She was a moment marker. A costume wearer. A decorator. By Easter, she'd have planned her costume for Halloween. On the Fourth of July, she danced around our yard with star-spangled flags poking out of her sun hat. For Thanksgiving, she stuck cupcakes together to make them look like turkeys. And she always thought of others. One Easter, she gave away her Easter basket to a child in her class whose parents couldn't afford one.

And the moment one holiday was over, she started counting down to the next. She loved them all and dragged us right into every one of her giddy celebrations.

Having Molly made me fall in love with the holidays too. Her love for them was infectious. Or maybe it's that she kindled something in me that had been there all along but that I'd shut down when my childhood didn't allow for it.

That's one of the beautiful things about having children, they get you to experience vicariously the things you missed out on as a kid.

I came to match every one of Molly's wacky holiday ideas with my own. My favorite was Easter. Before bed, I'd get Molly and Gracie to scatter jelly beans all over the lawn. When they were asleep, I'd go downstairs and pick up all the jell ybeans and plant lollipops where they'd landed. When the girls woke up the next morning and looked out of their window, they'd think that their jelly beans had sprouted overnight. Molly helped me maintain my belief in magic, and sometimes I turned conjurer myself.

The Easter before Molly died, I reminded the girls to decorate their trees. I noticed a beat of hesitation. Molly was thirteen. Gracie fifteen. Aren't we too old for this, they were thinking? "If you don't decorate your trees, the Easter Bunny won't come," I said, putting on as serious a face as I could manage. They looked at each other again and smiled. That night, their trees were decorated more beautifully than ever before and placed outside their bedroom door. Their baskets were filled.

At Christmas, Molly's spirit of celebration reached its peak. The dance recitals. The chocolate Advent calendars. The intoxicating anticipation of buying and wrapping presents and

decorating the house.

I remember watching her skipping down the porch steps and across the yard to catch the bus, the silver bell on her Santa headband jingling behind her. The December before she died, she wore that headband to school every day.

We were known for our yard decorations. Each tree limb and shrub was wrapped in strings of fairy lights. A huge inflatable Santa swayed where the Banzhoff Beach pool went in the summer. Banzhoff was Kenny's family name, the name the girls took. People took detours to drive past our house, just so they could see our decorations. Molly orchestrated it all.

Our last Christmas together was extra special. The year before had been tough. We'd been struggling with our family finances. Kenny and I were going through a rough patch. I hadn't done my part in making it special for the girls. So, this year, I promised myself I'd make up for it. Our yard was brighter than ever. I spent hours getting just the right gifts for the girls. Kenny took them shopping as well. They received everything on their lists. On New Year's Eve, Molly, Gracie, and I put our fists together and declared that 2016 was going to be the best year ever.

Five months later, Molly was dead.

Looking back, now, I sometimes tell myself that if I'd known that Molly would be leaving us so soon, I might have taken her aside and asked her to tone it down a little. *It'll help us survive when you're gone,* I'd tell her. Because all those moments now, we still have to go through them—only without her and her jingling Christmas headbands and her Fourth of July flags and her sheer joy at being alive.

Molly had teased us into falling in love with life and then, just as we caught onto the magic, she vanished, tripping the fuse box on the way out. And now, all we can do is to sit in the dark wondering whether there ever were lights in the maple tree or a skinny-legged little girl who jumped around with a red Santa headband on, a magical elf goading us into loving

life as much as she did. Maybe, we keep thinking, it had all been a dream.

For the next four years, we'd ignore every single holiday. I think we hoped that if we pretended it wasn't happening, Christmas and Easter and Halloween and Valentine's Day and Thanksgiving and the Fourth of July and Father's Day—and Mother's Day—would slink away and leave us alone. The holidays were our signal either to flee (one year we went to Hawaii, another to Disney World) or to hunker down under the covers and lick our wounds and curse the world for taking her away. Without Molly there, the holidays were just too much.

An image flashed behind my eyes. Mother's Day a year before. Molly and Gracie standing in the kitchen in dresses and aprons, waitresses welcoming me and asking what I wanted for breakfast. They had set up a restaurant. Created a menu. They were serving me. It was all Molly's idea.

As I lay on the living room floor a year later, I could hear through the window the traffic from the highway, already thick that morning. And it hit me all over again. I have to live in this world, a world without Molly while everyone else went on with their lives.

All week, I'd been in the surreal world of the hospital by Molly's bedside. I hadn't had to face the world outside. But now here I was, back in our home, lying on the living room floor, listening to the Sunday morning traffic, imagining all those people driving to their Mother's Day brunches. *All those people*, I thought. *They don't know. Everyone is living their life as though nothing's changed. And I have to live in that world.*

I got up off the floor, pushing away the thoughts and images spinning out of control around my head. I knew that I couldn't do this, that horizontal thinking was the worst thinking of all. I just had to get through this day, I told myself. Just this one day, without going crazy.

I got up, grabbed a coffee, and went to sit out on the porch. Sun streamed into the yard. It was the first sunny day all week.

Chapter 23

The Pink Casket

At some point in the day, Gracie and Kenny got up. The three of us walked around the house in a stupor. And then, the process that saves the grieving for a little while longer began: preparing for the funeral.

"I have Molly here," Glenn, the owner of Bennett's Funeral Home just down the road, said over the phone. "You can come and see her any time you want."

In the Bahá'í Faith, we don't believe in embalming the body, so there's no open casket. We're asked to bury the body no more than three days after death, before it starts to decompose. So, we had a few last days to see Molly, and then her body would forever be shut away in her casket.

Adults have their bodies washed in rosewater as a symbol of cleansing away this world in preparation for the next. Then the body is shrouded in simple cotton and cloth. It's about honoring the gift of life and preparing the soul for the next stage. But none of this applies to children. The sadness of the physical realm doesn't need to be washed from their bodies. The darkness of the here doesn't need to be gotten rid of to prepare the soul to move more easily from the body to the spirit realm. Children's bodies are still pure; they haven't lived long enough to absorb the pollution of the world.

I drove to the funeral home alone with Kenny. My mom

stayed home with Gracie.

When we arrived, Glenn talked me gently through all the details.

I picked out a pink casket. I knew that no one would see the color deep in the ground but I felt that Molly would know and that would make her smile. And it lifted my spirits too. If I had to think of Molly in any casket at all, thinking of her in a beautiful, bright pink casket somehow made it all a little more bearable.

Glenn gave me a quote; it was going to cost $3,500. Three thousand five hundred dollars for a box that would lie in the cold ground.

My heart sank. Our finances hadn't been in a good place for years.

"I thought children's caskets were free," I said, shocked that I was even having to think of money at a time like this.

"Well, Molly's tall," Glenn said. "She'll need an adult casket."

I don't know why this made me so angry. I wasn't angry at him. Glenn was kind. I was angry that once again, Molly was somehow being short-changed for something that was out of her control. So what if she was tall? She was thirteen years old. She'd only been thirteen years old for a few weeks. She was still a child. If children get free caskets, she should get a free casket.

"I know it's not your decision," I said. "But maybe you could call the company that deals with caskets? Maybe they'd understand?"

Earlier, Glenn had told me that the funeral would probably cost around $15,000 in total. We couldn't afford anything close to that.

It's a horrible truth that funerals are expensive. That thought makes me angry, that when you're going through hell because you've lost someone you love, you have to think about money. And it turns out that rich people, even when their lives are over, get a better deal than the poor. Our family didn't have much money then. Kenny wasn't working because of his kidney. We were still paying off his debts. I'd started a new teaching job a few months back, but that didn't pay much.

The $15,000 Glen quoted wasn't a high price; it was just enough to cover an ordinary funeral, no bells or whistles. It turns out that the mechanics of death are, quite simply, expensive. But to me, it all felt wrong. There should be provision for this, I thought, a common act of humanity that would take care of the dead without turning it into a financial transaction.

Glenn could sense my distress. He knew that I wanted this beautiful casket for Molly. And he knew that I couldn't afford it.

He pressed my arm. "Let's see what I can do," he said.

In the end, we got the casket for free.

As for all the other expenses, we somehow made it work. We had help from family and friends. Molly got the funeral she deserved. But there are millions who don't. Families like ours, who get into horrible debt, who have to scrimp and save or who have to pare down the funeral to its barest bones to be able to afford it. It shouldn't be this way. So many things, I was finding out, simply shouldn't be this way.

~

Glenn then took me to the room where Molly was being kept for visitors.

She was still in her johnny from the hospital. There was a cozy blanket covering her as well. Her eyes were closed and there was a sunken look behind her eyelids from where they'd been removed the night before. I thought about where Molly's eyes might be now and about how long it would take for them to put them into another living person. Was someone already looking at the world through Molly's eyes, I wondered? And what were they seeing? And was a bit of Molly with them in that gaze?

As I stepped closer, I realized that the Molly lying here was worlds away from the Molly I'd slept next to in the hospital only twenty-four hours before. On life support, she looked like she was sleeping. Her skin was soft and warm. There was a pink flush in her cheeks. Now, she looked gray. And when I touched her forehead, expecting the warm, smooth skin that I'd touched a million times, I felt something hard and cold and lifeless. In the many stages of Molly's death and my coming to terms with it, this was perhaps one of the first when I realized that her body was truly dead. Her skin felt like concrete.

I heard Gracie's voice in the lobby. She'd come over with my mom.

She ran into the room and as soon as she saw Molly, her face lit up. I felt like I was watching Gracie greeting Molly when she got out of school. Whenever they were apart, even if it was only for a few hours, they missed each other. Dread washed over me as I realized that Gracie was somehow expecting Molly still to be alive, that she was hoping to find her sister again like she found her hundreds of times, standing at the bottom of the driveway, greeting her after school.

Gracie had been with us at our local hospital and all through the last week at the children's hospital, and she'd been there when Molly was unplugged and the machines were switched off. But, like me, she still expected Molly to show up again.

Gracie walked over to Molly and reached out her hand to touch her. As she made contact with Molly's face she flinched and stood back. Her face instantly changed. She turned away from Molly, walked to the edge of the room, sat on a chair, and hid behind her phone.

She'd come into the room thinking that she was seeing her sister again and then she got closer and realized that it was a horrible trick, that it was just a body. A cold, hard body, pretending to be Molly. Looked at from a distance, the body looked like it held everything Gracie knew and loved about her sister, but close up, it turned out that it was a fake. That Molly wasn't there at all.

Except for Tuesday when we'd come back to dress Molly for the funeral, Gracie decided not to come and visit her again. It was too hard.

It was different for me. Glenn told us that we could come as often as we wanted, and I took him at his word. I spent those days before the funeral coming over again and again. Being with her even like this was better than not being with her at all. I didn't want Molly to be alone. And I didn't want to be without her either. In a few days, she'd be buried deep in the ground. Soon, I would never get to see her again.

At one point, my mother said, "Why are you fussing so much over that dead body?"

I was mad at her for saying that. Our relationship had been hard in the months leading up to Molly's death. Our relationship has always been difficult. We rub each other the wrong way. Perhaps I was mad because she could see it, that my life was falling apart. And because she could feel it too, in the way that mothers always do with their children, that something terrible was going to happen. But we never want to hear the truth of what's happening from our mothers. Or to have their judgment when we're suffering. I didn't want her to tell me that she knew Molly was sick. That she knew she was going to die. And I didn't want her here, telling me how to care for my dead child's body.

As a Bahá'í, my mother believed that Molly's soul was no longer here; her body, now, was just a shell. But she didn't get that, at that moment, Molly's body was all I had left. And that her body, even her dead body, mattered to me.

"Don't you get it, Mom? Those elbow dimples. I made them. Those knee crooks? I kissed them a thousand times. That soft belly? That was me too. No one other than me grew Molly inside their body. This is Molly. It's her body. It's part of who she is. And it matters to me."

This was the constant battle inside me, an understanding

of my faith and a belief like my mother's that Molly's spirit had left her body and a deep yearning for Molly's physical self.

Bodies matter. We live in our bodies. We give birth through our bodies to the bodies of our children. We hug them and smell them and stroke them, we brush their hair and celebrate them losing their first tooth. As mothers we know every line and curve and scar and texture as well as we know our own bodies; sometimes I think that I know my children's bodies even better than my own. And here she was, lying in front of me, her body, part of Molly, and I wasn't ready to just dismiss her as being gone, as it not mattering. I knew that once she was in the ground, I'd never see those physical parts of her again, that then I'd have only her spirit to relate to.

I wanted to be with Molly's body for as long as possible.

Chapter 24
Preparing for the Funeral

I was glad that the funeral would take place soon; it kept my mind busy and stopped it from going to the dark places it had in those first days after Molly's death.

On Monday afternoon, Glenn called to say that the casket arrived. He suggested we come down with some clothes for Molly.

I knew immediately what I wanted her to wear. I pulled the pink dress off the hanger on the back of my bedroom door. It hadn't moved from the place where Gracie had shown it to me early on Saturday morning, so excited by her trip to the mall with Molly. "She looks beautiful in it," Gracie had said. "You'll see."

We didn't know that morning that the first and last time I'd see Molly wearing that dress would be on her dead body in her casket, a pink casket to match the pink dress. Just like Molly hadn't known thirteen days earlier, when she twirled around for Gracie in the dressing room mirror at the Rocking-ham Mall, enchanted to have found such a beautiful dress, that she'd be wearing it sooner than she ever expected and that it wouldn't be to a party—or not the kind of party she could ever have imagined.

Thirteen days between when a young girl believes her whole future lies ahead of her, a complete trust that life will continue, to this, a dead body in a casket.

I still can't get my head around how it all happened. How this kind of thing can happen to anyone. How life can be so full one moment and extinguished the next.

We brought a cami for her, too, to put under the dress. It turned out that we couldn't dress her, not properly. That lifting her or bending or moving her limbs could break her skin. Glenn explained to us that when the body isn't embalmed, it starts to decompose. Those words hit me right in the gut, that her beautiful, smooth skin would break. I couldn't get my head around it: why would my baby girl break? I didn't want to live in a world where that was possible.

Glenn picked up on my distress. I guess he sees it a lot.

"My daughter will help get her dressed so that she looks beautiful," he said gently.

Both the cami and the dress had to be cut open. They were placed on top of Molly's body and pinned beneath her to the cushions of the casket. I realized then that we didn't give her shoes, that she went to her grave in bare feet.

We put a few things into the casket with Molly.

Her script of *Bye, Bye, Birdie*–she'd been in her Middle School play a few weeks before, a lead for the first time. She'd come home telling me that she'd found her people and her place. That she loved the theatre. That she wanted to be an actress.

A stuffed elephant that her best friend, Keisha, had made for her.

A golf ball from the games she used to play with Kenny.

A pair of her tap shoes.

Tokens from every religion I could think of. Every God and prophet. A cross. A small Buddha. Holy water and a nine-pointed star. Why not prepare her for every eventuality, I thought to myself. And it was more than that too. I believed in all these things, in the plurality through which the divine shows up in our lives. They were all valid. In one way or another, they would all take care of Molly.

Gracie put a necklace with half of a pendant that said "sisters" on it on Molly's' neck. She kept the other half for herself.

And then we put some lip gloss on her. A little blush on her cheeks. Some eyeshadow. We took pictures of her eyelashes, which were so pretty, a mile long. She wasn't the sparkly, living Molly we knew, but she still looked beautiful.

~

Tuesday was the last day I ever saw Molly. Lots of people had come and gone to say their goodbyes. Cathy, my sister-in-law, came by several times. She was wonderful in those days. While I walked around in a daze, she put together the graveside service. Whenever I needed her, she was beside me.

I kissed Molly one last time, and then Glenn closed the lid and explained that the next thing they'd do would be to suck all the air out of the casket. It preserved the body for longer.

I think of her now, lying in that casket. Perhaps, with no air to decompose her, she still looks much the same. I don't know the science of these things. But I do know that she won't have grown. That while today as I tell this story, her friends are eighteen, she's still and always will be thirteen. That although Derek, the boy she loved, is a foot taller now, she's still the same height she was when they shared their first kiss.

~

The rest of the day was taken up with other funeral details. We went to the cemetery, a mile from my house, to choose the plot where Molly would be buried. I'd wanted her close to the pond on a hill with lots of space around it, but whenever they dug down two feet, they hit granite and said it wasn't possible to put a grave there. So, we had to move her farther down.

Although we couldn't afford it, I ended up buying all the plots around Molly's grave. I wanted to have the space to give her a tree and a bench, the room for flowers to grow and spread. I didn't want her to be squeezed in among strangers.

After that, we went to Star Granite to choose her headstone. A former student of mine, Ricky Devoid, owned this place. Our backyards used to touch. All of us neighborhood kids loved his mother. I never imagined one day I'd be asking her son to make my daughter's gravestone. But I live in a small community. The house I have now is a mile from the one I grew up in. We all know each other.

Ricky did a beautiful job for us. We chose the words she'd put on her Instagram bio, as though she were writing her own epitaph, as though she knew that she'd be leaving us soon:

> *Do you think you have a purpose?*
> *If so, what?*
> *I think mine is to make people happy.*
> *Does that make you happy?*
> *Yes?*
> *Purpose Fulfilled.*

We struggled over choosing the date of her death. There were so many times that she died that week. In our local hospital. After the operation at the children's hospital. When they declared her officially dead on Thursday. Part of me didn't want to choose an end date at all. How could there be an end date to Molly?

Finally, we went with Saturday, the seventh, the day she was unplugged.

And then we drove home and waited for night to fall, and I lay back down on the living room floor with Gracie and, finally, sleep came. Tomorrow was her funeral.

Chapter 25

The Funeral

The week when Molly was in the hospital was hugely public. I'd invited everyone to come and spend time with her and to say goodbye. And there'd be time again later for big gatherings, but I wanted the funeral to be quiet, just my family and my closest of friends.

We arrived at the cemetery at around 10:00 a.m. Everyone from my side of the family came, even those who didn't have much money to cover their traveling expenses. My parents, my aunts, uncles, and cousins. My siblings. My sister-in-law, Cathy, sang and designed the program. Kenny only had his three children there from his previous marriage and his two best friends, Gary and David. There were a few notable absences: people who made excuses not to be there. It was too far. They were busy with something. I guess the people who were meant to be there were there.

There was a tent and chairs. The pink casket sat in front of us, elevated on a metal structure. Artificial turf covered the pile of dirt next to the grave.

I remember asking Glenn where Molly's head would be when she was put in the ground, and he explained that her feet would be toward her gravestone. I wanted to know for when I'd come to visit. In the weeks and months and years that followed, I'd come here again and again and lie on the grass next to her, facing the right way.

I'd told everyone to wear something pink to honor Molly's favorite color and to stop the funeral from being too somber. Gracie wore a white romper with a pink belt. Glenn from the funeral home wore brightly colored socks. He said he always did that for kids' funerals. I imagined a drawer in his home full of those colorful socks for all those dead children who are brought to him.

Just before the funeral started, Nathan, my uncle, who'd driven all night from Wisconsin, pulled into the cemetery. He and his wife, Julie, had lost their son when he was eight years old. I'd felt sorry for them and saw the death of their little boy as the most unbearable tragedy. But I hadn't understood, not really, not until now, the full scale of their loss. We're part of a club now, those of us who have lost children. No one else will ever understand. And that's fine with me. The fewer people who get it, the fewer people who must live through it, the better.

The service was organized by Cathy and me; we sang, said prayers, and shared stories. Gracie had a really hard time that day.

It was a nice funeral. Low key but right for that day, for us as a family. I invited Erin Howard, Skylar's mother (one of Molly's childhood friends), to come and take photos.

People find it odd sometimes, how I want to capture all the memories, even the sad ones. I guess it's my way of clinging in whatever way I can to what there is left of Molly. And the memories would be proof. That she'd been here, that we were a family who loved and lost their child.

I left before they lowered Molly into the ground; I couldn't watch. I remember feeling the panic of her being taken away from me, again. And how final it would be this time. She was closed in that casket, but she still felt close. Now she'd be down in the earth, far from where I could touch her. There were so many moments in those ten days when I had to let go; each one felt harder.

I walked away. I needed to scream. Cathy tried to come after me, but I heard someone say, "Let her go."

I was glad. I didn't want anyone.

I peed my pants. Like I did when the neurologist had said it was too late. Like I did in the chapel when the doctor said that the operation had failed to save her. It's one of the reactions my body has to losing control. A signal that things aren't OK.

~

After the funeral, we headed home. A friend who worked at Olive Garden had dropped off a load of food. I asked Lisa, a neighbor and friend who lived up the street, to set up the food. She worked as a waitress. I'd only asked her to be there when the food arrived but when we got back from the cemetery, she was still there and she was wearing her white shirt and her black apron. Lisa stayed the whole day, serving us. She said she wanted to do it. She's one of those spiritually connected people who knows how to be there for others when they're suffering. Who understands that sometimes going the extra mile is just the human thing to do.

At around 4:00 p.m., most of my family had left. There was still a ton of uneaten food. I looked out across the neighborhood and told Kenny that I wanted to invite people to come and eat the leftover food. I couldn't bear sitting around in an empty house staring at all those platters. So, we walked up the street and invited everyone we saw. I told them that we'd just buried Molly. That we weren't doing so well. That we had a load of food that needed eating. That we'd started up a fire pit in the yard that we could sit around as it grew dark. That we'd like their company.

They all said yes. They filled up our yard. And I remember thinking that this is how community should be, that easy, open-hearted, unquestioning coming together. We should do it more. Maybe then, we'd all feel less lonely. And it shouldn't take the death of a child to make it happen.

And I thought about Molly and how she would have liked it. How maybe she was the one, wherever she was right now, who made this happen. Maybe this was part of her purpose, her longing to make people happy.

Chapter 26

MollyB
The Musical

The graveside funeral was just for us as a family. But we knew that we needed more than this, an event to celebrate her life to which everyone whose life had been touched and made brighter by Molly was invited.

While we were still at the hospital, sitting next to Molly's bed, Kenny and I talked about what we should do to mark Molly's life. Something beautiful and joyous that represented all that she was and all that she loved. We came up with the same idea: a show.

Cindy, the head of Molly's dance school, was there that day in another room. We went out to see her and said we'd been thinking about what we could do to celebrate Molly's life and, before we had the chance to finish, she interjected, "A show."

It had to be a show. A beautiful performance on stage, with singing and dancing and acting and speeches and sketches and songs with as many of her friends taking part as possible. Because that's what Molly loved most.

So, on Thursday morning, the day after the funeral, I went to Cindy's house, and we started planning Molly's goodbye party, her musical.

Cindy is one of the most beautifully put together people I

know. She's approaching seventy, but her hair and her make-up are always perfect. And she's a professional. It matters to her that her shows are of the highest possible standard.

But this was different. She didn't care whether the people in this show were good at dancing or not or whether they'd had the rehearsal time or whether she'd manage to choreograph it all in under two weeks. This was about Molly. Only those who knew and loved Molly would perform. There would be no professional stand-ins to make the show look better. The sole purpose of this show was to celebrate Molly, who she was and what she loved.

"We'll run it like a recital or a competition. An adult or a student will talk between each act. We'll have a backdrop. We'll do what we can with the lights and the music ..."

Cindy's thoughts tumbled out. She took notes. Thoughts coming to her faster than she could record them.

The last time I'd seen her, she was standing in the hallway of the hospital, having said goodbye to Molly, bent over and crying and unable to make sense of what had happened. Like all of us, she needed to *do* something, anything, to distract her from the unbearable pain of losing Molly.

When Gracie first started dancing, Molly, two years younger, still a baby, sat on Kenny's lap through all the classes, watching her big sister. Gracie would come over and cuddle her all the time, so proud of her Molly. Cindy called Molly "Gracie's baby." As soon as Molly could walk, she started dancing too, one of the youngest to start at our local dance academy. It wasn't long before Molly was helping Gracie learn her steps.

Cindy had taught Molly to dance. And she'd watched her grow up into a young girl. Molly had been in hundreds of Cindy's shows and competitions and dance camps. Molly and Gracie probably spent as much time at the dance academy as they did at home. Cindy and the other teachers and dancers were like family to them.

Competition season was over, but recital season was just

beginning, and Cindy decided that Molly's musical would open the season. She called the local arts center, a 1,300-seat theater in town that Molly saw as her second home, and slotted an extra date into the dates for the spring show. The musical would take place on Monday, the twenty-third of May at 6:30 p.m., giving people time to get home from school and work and to have dinner.

There wouldn't be a single rehearsal. There wasn't time. Everyone just had to be responsible for their part and do their best on the day.

There were moments leading up to the show when I was worried that it wouldn't work. How could a show this big without any real preparation work? We only had eleven days. So many people wanted to be involved. How could it possibly all come together?

I'm still not sure how it all worked. Whether it was God or Molly or the universe. But somehow, the most amazing show that anyone in town had ever seen was created in under two weeks.

It's been seven years since that show. I thought that the memory of that day would grow smaller as things do over time. That I'd forget the details and all the feelings and the magic of it all. But some memories stay. The magnitude of that show and all those who performed and spoke and contributed, that beautiful celebration of Molly's life, is something that I will always carry with me. I wish that Molly could have been sitting in the seat next to me on the front row, squeezing my hand, her eyes big and bright and shining with excitement. I wouldn't ever get that again, her physical presence. But this I'm sure of: her spirit was in every second of that show. And she would have loved it.

It was incredible how everyone contributed to the show, even strangers.

When I went to print the programs at FedEx, they said it would take ten days to print them. When they found out I was

Molly's mom and saw what the program was for, they said they'd have them ready the next day and they wouldn't charge me. One thousand three hundred programs for free.

When I went to the pharmacy to pick up medication to calm my nerves, the pharmacists all said they were coming to Molly's show.

One of Molly's friends from orchestra had a dad who managed the Olive Garden in town. He got three local Olive Gardens to contribute all the food for the event.

A hairdresser friend did my hair along with my sister Eleanor's hair for free. I don't think I'd brushed my hair since the day Molly was admitted to the ER.

Cindy footed the bill for the show and orchestrated the whole thing. During the show, I caught a glimpse of her in the wings of the stage, her headset on askew, her usually perfect hair caught up in her microphone, the emotion raw on her face, fighting tears. She'd curated hundreds and hundreds of shows. She could do them in her sleep. But this one was different.

The only things I needed to cover financially were the curtain pullers and the lighting crew because they're unionized, but they all paid their salaries right back to the MollyB Foundation.

All those who worked at the Capitol Center for the Arts volunteered their time for the event. They served the food and ushered people to their seats.

There's so little anyone can do when a child has died. In the grand scheme of things, I mean. Most of all, they can't do the one thing that would make a real difference: bring your child back. But our small town pulled together in every way it knew how, to make us feel loved and supported and to celebrate the short and extraordinary life of our beautiful Molly.

The night before the show, I lay awake next to Gracie on the bed we had created on the living room floor. I was suddenly scared that no one would come. That I'd been foolish trying to make this big show. People wanted to move on with their lives.

It turns out that every one of the 1,300 seats of that auditorium was filled. And the rest of the people who came stood in the aisles and at the back and in the balcony.

The show opened with the competition piece that Molly, Gracie, and her friends had danced in only a few weeks before, "It's a Musical" from the comedy musical *Something Rotten*. It was Kenny's idea. And it was perfect. Funny and clever and brilliant, just like Molly.

I watched Gracie dancing, her costume sparkling, her legs tapping away, her bright lip-sticked smile. Her first time dancing without her sister there.

And I looked at the space that the dancers left on stage where Molly should have been. They did this for all the numbers that Molly had danced in or would have danced in for the coming spring recital. They'd leave this space for her again throughout their performances in the coming days. No one wanted to fill Molly's spot. No one ever could.

After that opening number, Kenny, Gracie, and I walked onto the stage. I wore a pink polka-dot dress and pink crocs. Kenny wore a pink polo shirt. Gracie was still sparkling in her sequined black-and-white costume.

I don't know how I managed to speak in front of all those people except that it's something I'm good at: stepping outside myself, putting on my educator cloak, and getting the attention of a room. It wasn't really me up there. Or not the me that had lost a child. I thanked everyone. I made a joke about how overwhelmed I was by people's love for Molly when often she'd been a pain in the ass for me.

I shared how everyone knew her as this kid who was kind and loving and who always reached out to those who needed her most. And then I said, "But I want you to know, she did not do that for me, ever."

I talked about what a challenging child she'd been. How, when she was two and still in diapers and already very articulate, she sat on the floor in our living room, fussing and whining. She'd been this way all day. Not happy with anything we gave her. By the end of the day, I was exhausted.

"Oh, Molly, all you've done all day is cry," I said to her.

She looked up at me with those huge eyes of hers and answered, "Well, maybe if you were doing your job better as a mother, I wouldn't be upset."

The audience laughed. They recognized this dynamic. How wonderful Molly was with everyone. And how adversarial, questioning, and testing she could be with me and her own family.

As I stood on that stage, sharing that anecdote about my brilliant and fierce little Molly, all the memories came flooding back.

Of how similar we were, which meant we drove each other crazy.

Of how many times we'd knocked heads.

Of how it made us love each other more fiercely and how sometimes it made daily life impossible.

"Do you want to be right or do you want to be happy?" was a mantra I repeated to Molly more times than I can remember.

It ended up being fifty-fifty. Sometimes she wanted to be happy, but just as often, she wanted to be right.

In every way imaginable, Molly was me. From her ability to read without being taught, to being a bit controlling and strong-willed, to walking so close behind me that I knocked her over whenever I stopped. My mother knocked me over hundreds of times because I walked so close behind her. Molly was always trying to catch up with me, she had questions, she wanted to find out what was going on beyond the world of her childhood.

Like Molly, I was keen on fairness and justice and would always bring it up. "Well, that's not right, that's not fair." I'd say, over and over as a child.

I always thought I was right and if I wasn't right, I had to find out what was right and make myself right. That was Molly.

There was another story I had wanted to tell that night on stage at the musical.

Molly, Gracie, and I were snuggled on the brown couch downstairs in the living room, reading a book. Kenny was out shooting pool. Molly and I begin arguing about the meaning of a phrase. It was a particular word or idea in the book that she was focused on. I can't remember the details now, only that she was adamant that she was right, and that I wasn't. She didn't express it that clearly. I misinterpreted her. She went on and on about being right and me being wrong. She wouldn't let it go. In the end, I just screamed at her, "I'm the adult, Molly. Just let it go!"

~

The argument followed us upstairs as we made our way to bed. She was trying to explain what she meant because I wasn't getting it.

"Enough, Molly!" I cried and threw the remote control at the wall. It shattered and sparked. Molly, Gracie, and I just stared at it lying on the ground, all broken, knowing it had gone too far.

"OK, I'll stop now," Molly said in a quiet voice.

We had a new clicker in the drawer. We got it out and set it up. She felt bad. She cried.

"Daddy's going to be upset. It's my fault the clicker's broken."

A few days later, she circled back to it.

"Mommy, what I meant was this," she said, and explained it clearly. It had been eating away at her for days.

"Oh Molly," I remember saying. "Why didn't you just say that at the time?"

Molly, like me, could be brutally honest.

She once told her friend Mykaila that she didn't like the birthday present she gave her. When I scolded her for it, she got mad. She thought that was so disingenuous. She had to work out the nuances of being truthful but not hurting others in the process. A path I still negotiate as an adult.

I still find notes and diary entries from her that describe how frustrated she is that I don't understand her.

The balance of all this is that every night, when the day was done, we'd snuggle up in bed with Gracie. And she always ran things by me when she wanted a serious question answered or needed help with something or needed something to figure out. Despite her frustration with me, she knew instinctively that we were alike. And that I was one of the few people who could answer her questions in a way that was honest and satisfying.

Dickens sums it best. With Molly and me, it was the best of times and the worst of times.

We were like magnets. We were the same, so we kept pushing each other away.

She was so often angry with me.

Before Molly could write, she told me, "I want to write my feelings down."

"OK," I said.

I gave her a piece of paper and a red and a black crayon. "These are the angry colors, Molly. You can use these to draw your angry feelings."

She covered that piece of paper in red until that crayon was a stub, and her little face was flushed with the effort.

Then she asked me to trace a big black circle in the middle.

She drew a stick figure of me in the circle with a line through it.

Molly wasn't afraid of telling me she hated me.

That week in Amsterdam, she was so angry at me for going off with Roy that she never answered my texts. I'd do anything to change that. To fill my phone with lovely words between us in those last days of her life. But that wouldn't have been true to how she was feeling about me and Roy or true to who she was. She had strong opinions. She knew what she believed to be right and wrong. And she'd make sure that everyone felt it and heard it. I wouldn't have had my Molly be any other way, even if it meant that sometimes I got hurt.

I wonder how we'd be now. She'd be twenty, an adult, more or less fully formed, ready to sail out into the world. Would we still struggle with each other? Would we be friends?

I blinked back into the present and looked out across the auditorium at those thousands of faces, children and families and friends who had known and loved Molly.

I smiled.

"I'm glad she was never like that with any of you," I said.

More laughter.

I wanted Molly to be remembered for the brilliant and beautiful and kind girl she was but I also wanted her memory to be real. She was a human being, a flawed one like the rest of us, who battled with herself and her mother and those she loved.

Kenny didn't say anything. He isn't a public speaker. I turned to Gracie, and she just said, "Thank you for coming everyone. I love you."

She gave a little bow and smiled.

She was buoyant that day, giddy with excitement at what we'd managed to pull together for her sister. I was glad that she had this time to feel some joy before the real grief set in.

And then the show began.

The Musical was made up of numbers that Molly had performed in or performances from people she admired. Her friends played instruments and sang and acted and spoke. There was a scene from her play, *Bye Bye Birdie.* Two dances that she'd been part of. Meaghan played the violin, Alyssa played the piano, Rachel and Mykaila sang. Her class made a video. Thirteen people who knew and loved her—friends, teachers, family—stood on the stage and talked about all the different aspects of Molly. Her kindness. Her creativity. Her humor. Her talent. How much she cared.

At the end of the show, they played a video made up of photographs from Molly's life.

My friend John spent the whole beautiful, sunny weekend

before the show inside, pulling together all my pictures to create the video. There were thousands of videos and photographs of Molly. I was big on documenting every memory we shared as a family. There was no way that I could pick out one photo of Molly and leave another. The task was beyond me. So, John stepped in.

Two songs accompanied the video.

The first was "22" by Taylor Swift, Molly and Gracie's favorite singer-songwriter. They had seen her twice in concert. Her lyrics capture exactly what young people feel and think. I smiled to myself as I watched the photographs of Molly coming up on the big auditorium screen: first-day-of-school photos with Gracie; recital photos in dance costumes; group photos from gymnastics meets; Molly with her violin at a concert, her eyes fixed on the conductor; Gracie and Molly in swimsuits at the Jersey Shore where we liked to vacation; endless, goofy selfies; birthday pictures, including one with a "13" candle from April, just a month before Molly died. There was baby Molly in diapers, still round and cuddly and big-eyed. There was cheeky toddler Molly running around the yard. And then, over time, there emerged my long-limbed, beautiful, swan-Molly, the one who commanded the stage in *Bye Bye Birdie*. Just before she died, she was on the threshold of growing up. I'd caught a glimpse of it, the beginnings of it, of the beautiful young woman she was meant to become.

I listened to Taylor Swift singing about being "happy, free, and confused" and about life being "magical and miserable." So much of that was true of Molly. She felt the bittersweetness of life. The happiest of memories with Gracie and me and Kenny and her friends. And all the hard, unfair, broken parts of life too.

And then the second song started. "For Good" from the musical *Wicked*. And that was perfect too in a way that was more profound. It spoke not of Molly's experiences, the ups and downs that Taylor Swift sang about, but about how our lives were affected by Molly, that her life and her death had changed us for good.

As I watched, I felt the full joy and beauty of Molly's life, of how she threw herself at everything in the way that people do in a musical. Her life was bright and bold and loud and color-ful and funny and deep. It was full of songs and stories. The fact that we were celebrating her life by putting her name in lights outside the Capitol Center for the Arts, the fact that we were celebrating her life not with a somber graveside funeral but with a musical filled me with joy. I knew that this was right for Molly. And I was grateful to have had a daughter who had lived so fully. Who had insisted that her life should be one great musical.

And I know, with every bone of my body, that all of us who had even the tiniest contact with this bright and beautiful life were changed for good.

But I was also overcome by grief because I knew that that space left on the stage between those dancers would always be there. From now on, whenever I looked out at the world, I would see that gap. When her friends performed their next show without her. And the one after that. When they cele-brated their birthdays and graduations. When they left home and went to college. When they got their first jobs. When they fell in love and got married and had kids. When, quite simply, they grew up, it would always be there, that shadow of a space where Molly should have been.

As I looked up at that stage, I wasn't sure whether I could live like this, forever reminded of that empty space where my beautiful, funny, impossible daughter should have been. When you have a baby, your life begins again, you reorient every part of yourself, every thought and hope and expectation towards the tomorrow of that child. And my child would have no to-morrows. That is why the death of a child is the most unnatu-ral of all tragedies. It disturbs the order of things. It turns the world on its head. It stops the clocks.

Joy and unbearable grief, those were my feelings as I sat in the front row of that theatre, looking up at that gap between the dancers. A gap which represented all the wonderful things that Molly had been and all those tomorrows that she would never see.

Both before and after the show, I was inside the theater, so I didn't get to see some of the magic that was happening outside. I was told later that people stopped their cars and asked what was happening and that others stood on the sidewalk, staring as hundreds of people all dressed in pink walked down Main Street toward the theater. They wondered what this could be about, who this could be for. I was glad. My overriding mission since her death is that Molly, in all her wondrous complexities, and what happened to her, should never be forgotten.

So many people wanted to stop and talk to me after the show that it took me awhile to get down to the lobby.

As I grabbed some food, many had left already. The lobby was nearly empty. I sat down at the closest table and saw four of the doctors and nurses who had treated Molly at the children's hospital. Chaz and Charlene were there as was Dr. Dennis and nurse Gina.

"I get it now," Charlene said, her eyes full of tears. "How amazing Molly was. How much she was loved. This should never have happened to Molly. She should never have died."

They told me that as they'd driven down the highway from the hospital, they thought they were coming to a middle school talent show. They had no idea they'd be watching a beautifully put together show at a theater packed with over a thousand people. They were overwhelmed by how many people loved Molly. By the impact she'd had on those around her.

There was a guest book put together by two of my cousins. I look at it now. All the signatures. All the messages of support. The memories, each of them so personal because that was Molly's gift. She embraced every individual who crossed her path and made them feel special for knowing her.

Everyone—*everyone*—who met Molly, was changed for good.

And then the auditorium lights went down, Kenny, Gracie, and I loaded up the car with a couple of leftover Olive Garden lasagnes and went back to our house to start our life without Molly.

155

PART III:

A STRANGE KIND OF JUSTICE

Chapter 27

In Real Life

Any fight for justice, especially when it comes to fighting for your dead child, is never as clean-cut or as satisfying a narrative as you see in the movies.

In real life, the lines between the victims and the perpetrators are blurred.

In real life, the legal process is less about truth and more about who can tell the most persuasive story.

In real life, there's rarely closure, much less a sense of victory. Everything is a compromise. But we knew we needed to fight for Molly, and the fight carried us through this stage of grief.

At the beginning of June, we received the pathology report, which revealed that Molly's brain tumor was benign. We'd suspected this from the start, but now we had the definitive biopsy results.

The roller coaster of grief and elation that I'd been through over the past month as we said goodbye to Molly, buried her, and then celebrated her through the musical, now turned to anger. Molly should never have died.

The day after the news, we went to collect Molly's medical files; from the children's hospital where she'd spent a week, unconscious, as we prayed for her to wake up; from the ER where she lain for sixteen hours; from her pediatrician's office, where she had visited multiple times.

We settled on an attorney, not only because of his professional expertise but because of his manner and his character, a choice I would be deeply grateful for.

And then the six long months of information gathering began.

Every photograph and video of Molly and us as a family that we'd ever taken.

Every essay and diary entry and letter she'd written. Her yearbooks. Her school reports. Records of her dance recitals, her theatre performances, her gymnastics meets. Crates and crates of objects and recordings that summed up my little girl's life with us.

Over a hundred interviews with friends, family, nurses, doctors.

Our attorney had a film created of Molly's life that represented who she was and what she meant to those around her and to the wider community. We booked a space in the local middle school auditorium and put out a message on Facebook inviting people to come and share their stories. We thought that a handful of close friends would show up. When we arrived, there were thirty people. The film producer said she was pleased at the turnout.

"This will help us make something good," she said.

"Just wait," I said. "I think more people will show up."

By the end of the filming session, we had filled the whole auditorium. Two hundred friends came to talk about Molly. Again, we were blown away by the love there was for Molly and by how much she'd clearly touched people's lives.

Information gathering was a long, draining process. Our attorney said that the case could take as long as five years. But in a way, I was glad. Just as the funeral and the musical had taken my mind off the unbearable grief of losing Molly, this process, too, helped me to find a reason to get up off the living room floor, it gave me a purpose to keep living. If we couldn't have Molly back, at least we could fight for her.

~

For legal reasons, there's little I can share about the process or outcome of the case. Much of it has been mentioned in the local press and can be found there. I wish I could say more because I think it could help people who find themselves in a similar situation.

I do, however, want to share this: the hardest part of the process, the part I wasn't prepared for, was how the process made me question myself as a mother. For a mother who is grieving deeply, who already feels guilt every second of every day about not having been able to keep her child alive, this felt like a particular kind of cruelty.

Think about your life. The things you've done right and the things you've done wrong. The things you're proud of and ashamed of. The things you'd go back and change and the things you hold up as victories, professionally and personally. They all form part of the mix of being human, of this journey that is life. We all acknowledge that we're a mix of all these things. And we trust that our best selves come out on top.

Now imagine looking at all those bad parts of yourself, those mistakes, the things you're ashamed of, through a magnifying glass. Imagine those things becoming the most important part of the story of who you are. How would you feel about yourself? How would any of us feel about ourselves under that kind of one-sided scrutiny?

I'd already put myself on trial. I'd already gone through every second of Molly getting sick, every second since the day she was born, trying to work out whether I'd missed something or whether I could have done something differently. And maybe there was something. A key moment, a turning point, that might have set events spinning off in a different direction, a direction that might have saved her. But that's not something I can ever know. Kenny and I did what all decent parents do. We observed our kids closely, we noticed when they were sick, we sought medical help when they were. We took them to their physicals. We found specialists when they needed it. We did what parents do. We cared for our girls as best we could.

The legal process made us question ourselves as parents and as human beings.

It all came out. Mine and Kenny's drinking. Kenny's debts. Our failed marriage. My relationship with another man. How I wasn't there when Molly was taken to the ER. I felt like it was my fault that she died from that tumor.

One of the most persuasive parts of the bad-mother narrative, was this: my drug addiction. It's hard to write about this. I know I don't like this version of myself. But I owe it to the story. To the mothers in America and all over the world, the women who live in Motherland and struggle with this too. Who know the truth that addiction is devastating. But there's another truth too: that addiction doesn't define you as a mother.

Being a mother means being completely present for every moment of your child's life. Regular drug and alcohol use stops you from seeing what's going on right in front of you. It makes you absent. Physically, because of the effect of the drugs, and mentally, as you're constantly finding excuses to leave your home and your family to chase down your next fix.

I've been clean for a long time now, and my sobriety has given me clarity and heightened my guilt. I believe that if I'd never got involved in drug use, I would have seen Molly's pain more clearly and somehow fought harder for her and she'd still be here today. Perhaps that's a delusion. Part of the guilt monster that chases me down every day. I guess we'll never know. But it's something I must live with.

This I know to be true: I am a flawed mother. A flawed human being. The things I have done that I shouldn't have done. The things I should have done that I left undone. I have made more mistakes than I can count. I have a lifetime of regrets and poor decisions. And I could have been a better mother to Molly and to Gracie.

Being married is hard. Being a parent is hard. Being a human being is hard. We get it wrong sometimes. Often. I never presented myself as a saint or as a perfect mother. If Molly were here today, she'd tell you about all the times I'd let her down. The times we'd knocked heads and fought. The times I'd driven her crazy and disappointed her. But she'd also tell you that I loved her and Gracie more than anyone in the world. She'd tell you that I always put them first and that I would never have done anything to hurt them.

She'd also tell you that my failures as a mother had nothing—*nothing*—to do with her death.

~

After years of fighting, there was no real resolution. What I can draw comfort from is that even though our fight wasn't world-changing in the way I'd hoped it to be, it formed part of those thousand tiny steps toward making parents aware of how to better advocate for their children. Every now and then, I hear a story that gives me hope.

A year after Molly's death, I was timing a track meet and a girl collapsed at the finish line. Someone called 911. I went over. The girl was struggling to breathe. Everyone was telling her to calm down, as if that was an option.

"We need to get her some space and some air, and we need to stop telling her how she should be feeling," I said.

I stayed with her until the ambulance arrived. Even then, she didn't want me to leave. She understood that I was on her side. That I wasn't questioning her pain.

Later, her trainer came up to me.

"Thanks for helping," he said.

"Sure."

"You know," he said, "my wife and I are physical therapists. We've been working with kids for years. But something's changed lately."

"In what way?" I asked.

"Have you heard about the story of the girl with the brain tumor? It's in all the papers. My wife and I have been following it. It's really been tearing us apart."

My chest tightened.

"What girl?" I asked.

"Molly, a girl called Molly."

Slowly, I unzipped my jacket. I was wearing my MollyB T-shirt.

"I'm her mother," I said.

He looked at me, stunned.

"My wife and I realized that perhaps we've been letting our young athletes down. That when they get hurt or complain about struggling with something, we've often dismissed them for being emotional or dramatic. And we're good people, just trying to do our jobs well, but we let them down. We're trying to change that now. To do better."

I loved everything about that conversation. That Molly's death had some impact on how they were doing their work. And more than that, that this man, this trainer, had just told me about Molly's story, without even knowing who I was. Molly's story was spreading, and it was saving lives.

Chapter 28

Our First Doctor

I will always be grateful to the doctors who cared for Molly at the children's hospital.

And I will always be grateful to the doctor who was there on the day Molly was born. A young doctor who did everything right. A doctor we loved. The doctor who suffered most because of Molly's death.

We first met Dr. Nick as Gracie's pediatrician a few days after she was born.

He was young, he'd only just started working in our town. He had brown, curly hair and wire-rimmed glasses and a kind face and he'd just had his first baby, too, with his wife, so he understood on a human level what Kenny and I were living through.

I warmed to him right away as did baby Gracie, whom he examined with tenderness and care. Right away, I trusted him to take care of my new baby girl.

And then, two years later, Molly showed up. He came to visit me shortly after I'd delivered her, and Kenny took a video of him peering down at teeny tiny Molly, a smile on his face, saying, "Hello, Molly."

~

And then he did all the things. He looked in her ears and her eyes and listened to her heart and rotated her tiny hips, making sure that she was healthy in every way.

We could tell that he loved his job. That he loved children. And their parents too.

As the girls grew older, and because their birthdays were just a month apart, we started doing their physicals together. They always looked forward to going to see Dr. Nick as they liked to call him. They laughed and joked with him. And when they talked about their bodies or their pain or something that they were struggling with, he took them seriously.

Over the years, Dr. Nick became an extension of our family. I knew that when I brought the girls to him, he would listen to them and take care of them like he would his own children. And he listened to me too. When I lost my job. When I was going through a hard time. He understood that a mother's care is intricately bound up with the care of her children. When my runners did well, he read about it in the paper and praised me as a coach. He was a deeply humane doctor.

In 2015, when Molly and Gracie were twelve and fourteen, the last physical they'd ever have with him, he asked them if they had boyfriends yet, and they screwed up their noses and said, "No—ew!" and they and Dr. Nick fell about laughing. We had a blast.

As is common practice with teenagers, he measured them against the SPENCA anxiety scale. He asked them whether they were stressed or anxious about anything and they told him, "Of course, we're stressed and anxious: we're teenage girls! Everything about being a kid right now is stressful. And we're busy. But it's OK, we're happy."

The four of us talked about good kinds of stress and bad kinds of stress. It was a lovely, open, mutual conversation of the kind I wish doctors everywhere had with their patients, whatever their age.

Dr. Nick was a trained pediatrician.

The girls had lived for over a decade in their own bodies.

There was an understanding that he wasn't the only expert in the room. And that the best kind of care came from a mutual respect for what both the patient and the doctor bring to the table.

He made a note in Molly's file that her anxiety levels were a little higher than Gracie's. But that wasn't a big deal. And for anyone who knew the girls, it would have made sense. Gracie has always been a happy-go-lucky, go-with-the-flow kind of girl. Molly was more anxious. She questioned everything; she wanted to get things right. It wasn't a condition, it was who she was, a part of her personality.

She's an anxious teenage girl, that's why she's having headaches.

She told them that she wasn't anxious, that she was in pain. That this wasn't about being stressed or busy.

In my moments of believing that Molly died for a reason, that somehow it was part of some purpose that is beyond my understanding, I think about how strange it is that Dr. Nick was absent for all of Molly's appointments between February and May 2016 when she had those terrible headaches. Which is why Molly's death was so devastating for him. That he wasn't there for her when she needed him most.

The week when she was on life support, Dr. Nick came to visit Molly and to say goodbye.

He sat by her bedside and took her hand and broke down. His crying reminded me of the way Molly cried, uncontrollably, nose and eyes running. There was something so vulnerable and childlike in how he just let all his emotions about losing Molly out like that.

Watching Dr. Nick sobbing next to Molly's life-supported body, the body he'd held a few days after her birth, the little girl he'd watched grow, the girl he'd given shots to and examined whenever she was sick with strep or a cold, the girl he'd joked with in his office just a year ago, it struck me that the quality that made Dr. Nick such a good doctor wasn't his medical training or his skills or his experience in pediatric care. It was his humility. And his willingness to be vulnerable.

A man who's prepared to show his brokenness at the death of his patient and the complex feelings of loss and guilt and disbelief and anger is exactly the kind of doctor we all need.

Dr. Nick slipped his hand out of Molly's, stood up, gave me a hug, and then he left.

And we buried Molly.

And I didn't see him again until, suddenly, I noticed on my calendar that the girls' physicals were coming up on the sixteenth of June, one month after Molly died.

I couldn't face going back to that office with Gracie. And Molly was dead, she didn't need a doctor anymore.

There are so many things that are lost when a child dies. Ripples that spread out from that death for decades. A thousand additional blows and losses.

Gracie loved Dr. Nick. She was devastated that she wouldn't get to see him again and that he wouldn't be her doctor. She and Molly were meant to be his patients until they were at least eighteen. He was meant to watch them grow up and graduate and leave for college.

When a child dies and your whole life is turned upside down, you cling to every little bit of consistency and normalcythat you can. That's why we didn't touch Molly's room. Why we didn't take her and Gracie's dance costumes off the stairs. A tiny bit of familiarity and continuity are comforting when nothing feels the same. Having Dr. Nick care for Gracie, especially at a time when she was so broken and vulnerable, would have been of deep comfort. But that too had been taken away from us. From her.

~

I could have just canceled the appointment. But something in me wanted to see Dr. Nick one last time. So, I kept the appointment. Not for Gracie or Molly but for me. Because I needed to talk to him one last time.

It was a beautiful, sunny day. When I arrived at the doctor's office at 9:00 a.m., the receptionist said that Dr. Nick had cleared his schedule that morning so that he could be available for me as long as I needed.

We grabbed a coffee and sat at a picnic table across from the parking lot and talked for three hours.

We talked about the good times. How much the girls loved coming to see him. What a blast we'd had a year ago as they joked about boyfriends and being teenagers. A million anecdotes from when they were babies to when he'd last seen them as young women.

And we talked about the sad things too.

About how terrible it was to lose a child.

About how, for both of us, in different ways, life would never be the same again.

I'd lost my daughter. My life as a mother had changed forever.

And the happy, young doctor we'd first met when Gracie was born, he was changed too. Molly's death had made him rethink his role, and the optimism he'd had only a year ago had gone.

~

I bumped into him again years later during a multicultural festival in town. His hair had turned gray. He looked tired and haggard. I asked him how he was doing.

"Not so good," he said. "How about you?"

I gave him a small smile and shrugged.

"Not so good."

When a child dies in the way that Molly died, more lives

are affected than we ever know.

I hugged him goodbye. I hoped that having his wife and three sons helped. I hoped that he would keep believing in himself as a doctor because the world needs more doctors like him. Good doctors.

PART IV:

HOW I LIVE NOW

Chapter 29
Sitting in the Rubble

I knew that Molly was dead. That she was never coming back. But there was something about spending those two years immersed in all of Molly's memories, in those hundreds of documents of her life with us as a family, in being caught up in the legal case, that somehow stopped me from having to face the full reality: she was gone, for good.

I had this sensation that maybe if we retraced the steps often enough, if we could identify exactly when a different decision or action could have been taken, then maybe there was still the opportunity of saving her. It was a trick of the mind that kept me believing that somehow we could still bring her back to life.

When the case was closed, that's when everything got really hard. Because now it was over. Really over. There was nothing left to do. No more funerals or memorials or legal battles. There was just life without Molly.

And there's something else that happens over time for grieving families, the rest of the world begins to forget and to move on in a way that you never will.

Molly died at the beginning of May 2016. A few weeks later, it was summer vacation. For those four months, we were barely ever alone. And during the court case, we weren't alone either. The busyness of gathering evidence and fighting back against the hospital's accusations against me and the legal team itself, which became an extension of our family, kept us from feeling the full force of Molly's death.

But now, Molly was buried, and the boxes and boxes of legal files were closed and it was just us. Me, Gracie, and Kenny. And we had nothing left to do but to face the full force of our grief.

I think often about how the Red Cross swoops in after a natural disaster, a hurricane or an earthquake or a tsunami. For days, sometimes weeks, they drop food and water from the sky. They send in trauma counselors. They offer practical and emotional support. The story of the disaster is beamed across the world. Millions of dollars are raised.

Every morning, that long summer after Molly's death, I'd wake up on the living room floor where I slept with Gracie, I'd grab a coffee, and head straight out onto the porch. I didn't want to give my brain the time to go to where it always went when I woke up, the panic at Molly not being here anymore.

The porch was filled with food. Every morning, there'd be another platter of lasagne or macaroni and cheese and pies and flowers and cards. And then the yard started filling up. My friends dropped by and sat with me for hours. And Gracie and Molly's friends filled our yard. Kenny and I somehow found the energy to fill up the pool that Gracie and Molly loved so much. The kids would just hang out all day in swimsuits and towels, sitting on chairs, being with Gracie, eating food and talking.

They gave us a grace period. A window of time when we didn't have to face the fact that we somehow had to find a way to start living again without Molly. The summer has a different rhythm for all of us, a kind of timelessness. We let it carry us through that first phase of grief: the shock and numbness and denial that this has really happened.

For Gracie, it was an incredible time. She and Molly had always struggled with the popularity battles at school and at dance. They knew they weren't ever the most popular kids in the room, but they weren't the dorky kids either. Secretly, they both longed to be the center of their friends' attention in the way that all teenagers do.

This was Gracie's moment. For the first time in her life, everyone was coming to her house and asking how she felt and wanting to hang out with her, ready to do anything for her. They were her Red Cross support team. She admitted to me recently that she loved the attention. That it made her happy. And it stopped her from thinking about Molly.

Even after the summer, when we felt the first signs of people returning to their old lives, while we were still flailing without Molly, we were distracted. Gracie found going back to school hard. It was the first time she didn't stand in front of our porch door holding a sign with Molly, backpacks on shoulders, eyes shining, wide grins. She was setting off on this new school year on her own as the girl with the dead sister. But even then, it was easier than what came later. The memory of Molly's death was still fresh in people's minds, Gracie's friends, our family, and community. They continued to look out for us. To make allowances. They understood when we broke down. They were patient with us. And the long hours of work on the legal case kept us busy too. We—and Molly—hadn't yet been forgotten by the natural relief teams. Not yet.

But then the weeks turned into months and the months into years. The seasons passed. The cold New England winter melted into spring and another summer, our second without Molly. A series of harrowing memorials: her absence for her fourteenth birthday, Gracie's sweet sixteen celebrated without her sister, remembering that horrible day when Molly was taken into the ER, the long week at the children's hospital, unplugging her, the funeral.

Then we fought our case.

And suddenly, something shifted. I could feel it physically. Someone, somewhere decided that it was time to draw a line under the death of Molly Banzhoff and move on. It was time for everyone to go back to their normal lives. It was time for the Red Cross to pack up and head to the next disaster.

And we were left, the three of us, me, Gracie and Kenny, sitting in the rubble. Roy was out of the picture, for now at least. My divorce from Kenny was no longer relevant. We stopped renting the apartment. We were a family again, which is what Molly always wanted. Only she wasn't here anymore. And if it hadn't been for her death, this new, cobbled-together family, a family held together by little else than the fragile threads of grief, would never have existed. And yet, as fragile and unlikely and thrown together as we were, we found strength in each other. If we were going to get through this, we had no other option but to draw close and to hold on tight.

The food packages stopped.

The cards and flowers now only came rarely.

People left our yard and didn't come back.

And now, whenever I mentioned Molly in conversation or posted a picture of her on Facebook or expressed outrage at how she'd been treated, I felt people take a step back. Enough, already, they were thinking. It's time to move on. It's time to get back to living. It's time to step out of the rubble. We've been good to you, we've listened to you and cried with you and sat with you and mourned with you, but we're tired now. We don't have the energy for this anymore.

I'm part of several online grief groups, mostly of parents who've lost children. We share thoughts and quotations. We support each other in a way that those who've never lost a child are unable to do. Recently, someone shared these words, "When people grow tired of hearing about our loved ones who've passed away, I just wish to remind them, we grow tired of having them dead."

We didn't know it then, that we hadn't yet been through the worst. Nowhere close. Over the coming weeks and months and years learning to live without Molly would get harder, not easier.

Chapter 30

How to Grieve

In the months and years that followed, I found different ways of managing my grief. Some of them helpful. Some of them destructive. They were all about survival.

Early on, I understood that I needed to find a place to scream.

Every animal finds a way to scream. It's a kind of primal necessity. We accept that from the animal world, yet somehow, we've lost a tolerance for human screaming. People who go around screaming their lungs out are considered dangerous or deranged; society quickly lets us know that we should keep our screams on the inside.

But screaming on the inside doesn't work. It might keep the neighbors from talking, but it doesn't do much good to our hearts. I have a suspicion that screaming, kept in, eats away at the most vital parts of ourselves. I think that not being allowed to scream is one of the reasons people turn to drugs and alcohol, anything to numb the unbearable pain that's trying to find its way out of our minds and our bodies and our souls.

We need to scream. I wish we were allowed to do it more. I wish there were screaming clubs and ceremonies, days of the month set aside for it. A place for us to let out our hurt and anger against the world.

I believe that a guttural scream in all its energy and noise is the deepest reaction a person can have.

When something is so unbelievably painful that it just can't be held in, when the anger or the terror or the panic or the sadness has built up to such an extent, there's nothing left to do but to scream. It's a way of surviving. And a way of signaling to ourselves and those around us and to the wider universe that things are not OK.

And screaming comes not only from pain and bewilderment and sadness but also from anger. Which is another thing we don't allow ourselves to feel, or not publicly. Anger is often the last thing for me. I go through the whole range of other emotions too. I don't give myself permission. But like screaming, I think it's necessary.

The poet and Northern Ireland peace negotiator, Pádraig Ó Tuama warns us about the danger of moving on from anger too fast:

"There's all kinds of reasons why we get caught in anger," he says. "And anger is a magnificent and important defense. And if forgiveness is ever to happen, there needs to be a level of safety. And sometimes anger is a reminder that safety hasn't been achieved yet, so anger is the protection. And anger has a deep intelligence in that moment."

I love that. That anger is a "magnificent and important defense," and that it has a "deep intelligence."

I was still deeply angry at the doctors who I believe failed to save Molly. At myself for not doing more. At the universe for taking her away from us.

And I needed to feel that anger.

And I needed to scream.

For me, in those months and years after Molly's death, screaming felt like the only way to survive.

I'd get into my car and just drive and scream. I had a towel on the driver's seat because sometimes, as I drove, I screamed so hard, I'd pee. I smelled quite a bit like pee during that time. I didn't care. I didn't care what I smelled like or that my hair wasn't washed or that I'd been wearing the same clothes for weeks. Most days, I didn't care if I survived. There were times when I'd drive as fast as I could without my seat belt on, goading the universe to take me too.

But then I remembered Gracie and buckled up again. If it weren't for Gracie, I'm not sure I'd still be here today.

Lying on the bed in the living room next to Gracie, I'd drift in and out of sleep. And the nightmares would come. One in particular. I dreamt that I'd lost Molly. That she wasn't in the house or in the hospital or even at the cemetery. That somehow, she'd disappeared altogether.

I'd wake up in a sweat, my heart thudding against my rib cage, terrified that she'd vanished altogether. Worse, that maybe she'd never existed.

I pulled on my sneakers, grabbed the car keys, and drove straight to the cemetery. I stood in front of her grave in my pajamas and read her name out loud. I was scared that someone might have taken her or wiped her name off the headstone.

Then I lay on the night-cold grass, remembering to place my body in the right direction so that we were facing each other. And relief flooded my body. She wasn't alive. Nothing could make her alive again. But at least she was here. At least she wasn't lost.

When I'd lain on Molly's grave for a while, reassured that she was still there, under the grass and the blossom tree in her pink casket and her pink dress, I'd pick myself up and get back in the car and drive to my screaming tree.

I always did the same loop.

Exit 9 on Route 89. Through Warner, Webster, Boscawen.

I'd find a clearing somewhere on the side of the road and I'd find a tree and hold onto it and scream at the night sky until I felt like my eyeballs were hemorrhaging.

By the time I got home, my voice would be gone. Kenny would ask me where I'd been and what I'd been doing. When my voice came back, I tried to explain. At first, he didn't understand. He wasn't the type to scream.

But then, one night, when I felt that his grief was too much to hold, I brought him with me. I took him to the woods. I guided his hand to the trunk of the tree to steady him. And I taught him to scream. I went first. And then I told him to join me. And then, he understood.

I tried to teach Gracie too. That screaming was OK. Necessary even. She's not as articulate as Molly. Words don't come as easily. When I recognized that she needed to say something but couldn't express it, I told her to just scream.

Once, I heard her screaming from the bedroom she used to share with Molly. She still didn't sleep in there, but she'd started going in every now and then to look at it. To remember the life she shared within those four walls with her sister.

Another time, at the end of the dance year, Molly's name was left off the back of the T-shirt. I've never seen Gracie so mad. She screamed and screamed and screamed. About the fact that the world was moving on when she couldn't. About the fact that Molly was never coming back.

Sometimes, I left her alone to scream. I gave her the space she needed to let out those deep, animal sounds of pain.

But mostly, I'd find her and hold her and tell her that it was OK, that screaming was good, that she needed it. That Molly would understand. That it was our way of surviving.

~

There's a reason the screaming took place at night on the side of the road in the dark woods of Boscawen rather than in my front yard. I knew that people didn't want to see it. Not anymore, anyway.

They might have forgiven me a few screams when the doctors delivered the news that Molly was never going to wake up and that we had to take her off life support. They might even have tolerated a scream at her funeral or through the legal case. But now, especially now, years later, I felt it loud and clear: it's time to put my grief away. It seems there's an expiration date on grief. A moment when you're expected to put your sadness about your dead child to one side.

And so, another way I learned to cope with my grief was to draw close to those people who understood, or at least who didn't judge me, who gave me time, who didn't expect me to get better and move on, and to take some distance for those who couldn't tolerate my sadness. Who expected me to be over Molly's death already.

Not that it was always easy. When I found an excuse once, for not wanting to join in with an event of some kind, a so-called friend said, "You can't keep playing the dead-kid card, Barb."

Maybe she meant well. Maybe this was what tough love looked like. But she was wrong.

A mother never gets over losing a child and she should never be expected to.

There's not much that will make me end a friendship. I'm loyal. I have too many flaws of my own not to be forgiving of other people's mistakes. But there's one thing I can't abide: the criticism that those of us who have dead kids shouldn't bring them into the conversation. To be honest, I think that every grieving parent *should* have a dead-kid card to play whenever they damn well please. If the worst thing in the world has happened to you, you get to do that, no questions asked.

You get to stay in bed rather than going to work because your child *is* dead and you can't imagine getting through another day without them.

You get to argue a case at a school board meeting about COVID because your kid is dead and you don't want any other kids to die because of careless decisions.

You get to cry when a ladybug lands on your arm because your dead kid loved ladybugs even if it's five years after your kid died.

You get to drink and binge eat and watch too much pointless TV because it's the only thing that will numb the pain of your kid being dead.

You get to not wash your hair for a week and hang around in food-stained pajamas because getting dressed and washing seems pointless when your kid won't ever wake up again.

You *get* to do those things. All of them. And more.

The truth is that most of us who have dead kids try really hard to get by each day without playing the dead-kid card. We brush our teeth and make our dinner and drive our cars and do our jobs and say polite things to strangers in stores and act like normal people rather than broken people. But we shouldn't have to.

We get to play the dead-kid card. Playing the dead-kid card is part of how we grieve. How we survive. And we get to play it as often as we want to.

Because the dead-kid card trumps every other card in the whole damn deck.

Some of these people who wanted me to move on meant to be kind, I'm sure. The subtext was that if I tried to forget, if I tried to move on, it would stop hurting so much.

I don't want to stay stuck in the horrible emotional mess of trauma. I want to get better. To get stronger. To move on with my life. To heal. But again, doing that means letting go of Molly, of who she was and who she was meant to be and *that* she was meant to be. And so, moving on feels like a betrayal.

Grief is living in a thousand and one paradoxes that have no answers.

A longing to forget alongside the fear of not remembering.

A longing to move on alongside a fear of the vacuum that will be left behind if I let go.

A longing for the pain to ease alongside a fear that it's the pain that's keeping her alive.

Because if I forget, if I move on, if I erase the pain, where does that leave Molly?

And there's another reason why grief doesn't just go away. When you lose someone, you're changed, not just because of the aching emptiness left behind by the person who's gone, the person you loved with every part of yourself but because their death reminded you that bad things happen and that they can happen again.

Most of us go about our daily lives largely ignorant of tragedy. It's hushed up and hidden away and, most of all, it happens to other people. Other people get cancer. Other people lose their jobs and their money. Other people go to jail. Other people are poor and homeless. Other people have their kids die.

I'm a realist. And I had my fair share of hardships growing up. But it wasn't until Molly's death that I realized quite how fragile life was. Now that this had happened, the worst thing imaginable, I realized that *anything* could happen.

I remember saying to Meaghan's mom, Sarah, on that Monday morning when we first arrived at the children's hospital, thinking that Molly might still make it, "I don't want to be the mother of a dead child."

I said it because I couldn't ever believe that that would be me. That this would happen to me.

But it did.

And so now, other things can happen too.

Something could happen to Gracie. Or to Kenny. Something terrible. Molly's death doesn't give us immunity from other bad things happening.

There's that saying, isn't there? "Lightning doesn't strike the same place twice."

Only it can. The saying is a lie. We believe it because we've said it or heard it so many times that it's taken on the guise of truth. And because we *want* to believe it. Believing in these clichés helps us get through life, it helps us deceive ourselves that it's all going to be OK, that there is some kind of rule of fairness, that there's some justice and balance and sense and order to it all.

I'm not a pessimist. In fact, by nature, I'm one of the most optimistic, positive, upbeat people you'll meet. I've been told that I have a gift for motivational speaking. For helping people, especially young people, believe in themselves. But grief has changed me. It hasn't made me negative or bitter or unwilling to believe in the goodness of the world or its miracles. But it's made me more prepared for an onslaught that will, in one form or another, at one time or another, suddenly and un-expectedly but inevitably come. A disappointment. A trauma. An unbearable loss. It's also put me on my guard. Having one dead child hasn't given an armor against any of this; in fact, it's done the opposite. You might think that when the worst thing happens, you can take some comfort from the fact that at least, now, you've hit rock bottom, it can't get any worse. That nothing like this will ever happen again. But that's not true. Life just doesn't work like that. Bad things can happen again and again. And worse things can happen even when you think that you've had your fill, your quota, that surely light-ning won't strike in the same place twice.

Only it does. All the time. Lightning can and often does strike in the same place, repeatedly, especially if it's a tall or isolated object. The Empire State Building is hit about twen-ty-five times per year. The difference is that, in life, you don't need to be particularly tall or isolated or exceptional to be struck again. Life isn't as discriminating as lightning.

Molly's death has taught me that anything can happen to anyone at any time. And so, alongside the grief comes the fear, which also keeps me from being able to move on in a way that those who have never faced something like this just can't understand. But alongside that fear comes a kind of clarity and strength, a kind of knowing, an understanding of what life is really like. And with that comes a truer way of being in the world.

There are hundreds of other ways, big and small, that formed part of my new, grieving landscape.

For a long time after Molly died, I didn't wear my seat belt. Which was foolish and dangerous. But I didn't care much about foolishness or danger. I didn't really want to be alive; if a road traffic accident took me, I wouldn't have to keep living here anymore without Molly. So, I let the seat belt ding play its song over and over and over. People who were in the car with me found it unbearable. Which is the point of the ding; it's so irritating that you're forced into putting your seat belt on. I found it comforting. It numbed me. It stopped me from thinking, which was a relief.

I changed the geography of my life too.

When you live in the same house and the same community, when you're a mother and a teacher and a coach, you take the same routes every day. You drive down the same streets and past the same buildings and landmarks. And when you have children, so, so many of those landmarks are associated with them.

There were places I simply could no longer go.

I couldn't drive past the park at the bottom of our road, which Kenny took the girls to almost every day of their childhoods.

I couldn't drive past the middle school where Molly was meant to be going into eighth grade.

I couldn't drive past the hospital where she'd died.

I had to re-orient my life and my body because there were some places and some pieces of music and activities that would steal away any little piece of strength I had to keep going.

And the worst place was the house. And there was no getting away from that.

The refrigerator is covered in pictures of Molly and Gracie. Their dance show pictures. Christmas card pictures. Poems and letters and Post-its. Our whole world was on there.

The bedroom the girls had shared, still full of Molly's stuffies and clothes and bedsheets.

The kitchen table where we'd eaten together as a family for thirteen years of Molly's life.

The brown couch the girls had slept on as babies and sat

on watching movies and played on and jumped off and snuggled on.

The back door where I'd take pictures of the girls at the beginning of every school year, holding up pieces of paper with the grades they were going into. I had to fight to take the last picture. Molly was going into seventh grade; Gracie was starting high school. They were too big for this kind of thing.

"You'll look back on this in years to come and be glad I took it," I said.

Molly will never get to look back. Or not in the way I thought she would. And looking at those photos is too much for Gracie, too, because she knows that every new school year or college year she starts now will be without Molly at her side.

Then there was the yard. The white fence that Molly and Kenny had started fixing the week I was in Amsterdam.

The patch of sand where we put up the pool every year.

The maple tree with the swing Molly loved.

The little path in the woods, the enchanted forest I'd made for the girls.

Every corner of the house and the porch and the yard reminded me of Molly and made living there unbearable. But it was our family home. The only home Gracie knew. And for all the pain, we didn't have the strength to move. So, we just existed there, trying not to look too hard or to feel too much and when it all got too much, we went away.

Not to the Jersey Shore, which was where we spent our family vacations. A beautiful strip of coastline which we loved. A place where we took hundreds of photos of the girls running into the sea and wearing their swimsuits and doing cartwheels on the sand. We would never go back there.

We'd go to Hawaii. And Disney World. Anywhere Molly hadn't been.

And then there was the worst thing of all: my own body. Perhaps it's because grief is such a physical thing. Because I was so exhausted. Because I'd spent so much time with Molly's dying body. Or because my mothering had been so much about physical touch and, in some ways, I'd died as a mother, and so that part of me had died too. Or maybe it went back further than that, to the little girl who was touched inappropriately, told to keep it a secret, and who felt such shame about what had happened to her that she would relive it repeatedly in most of her relationships. It's probably a bit of all those things. But after Molly died, I couldn't bear for anyone to touch me. I pulled away from hugs. When Kenny put a hand on my back, I cringed and pulled away. And worst of all, when Gracie came to me, needing to be held and snuggled, I felt as though I just couldn't. It felt like chewing glass. Most of the time I pushed down my discomfort, knowing that she needed me but, some of the time, I found a reason to push her away. And it wasn't about her. From when she was a baby, Gracie was soft-fleshed and warm and felt so, so good to cuddle. It was my body that was the problem. A body that had seen and felt and experienced too much. I needed physical space. I needed my body to be my own.

So, everything changed. My internal and external geography. My relationship to sound and music and touch and exercise. How my home, a home where I had nurtured my babies, now felt like a dangerous place. My ability to receive and give love, in any form, had vanished. It was like I was learning to live again from scratch, only I hadn't had nine warm, nurturing months in the womb to prepare me for this raw, loud, overwhelming world I was meant to navigate. I'd come through hell. And now I needed to live on earth. And no part of me knew how I was meant to do that. Or whether I'd survive it.

Chapter 31
Gracie

"I'm still here, Mom," Gracie says.

She says it when she feels that my grief is so overwhelming that I can no longer see what's in front of me. When she feels like I no longer see her.

You have a living child, Mom. That's what Gracie wants me to remember.

And the world reminds me too.

"You have Gracie," my friends and family say. Even people who don't really know me say it.

This is the subtext:

I should count my blessings. Be grateful for what I have. Acknowledge the gift of my one, beautiful, living child.

And I am grateful. Every single moment of every single day, I'm grateful for Gracie. My sweet firstborn who is such a kind and gentle, beautiful soul who has lost so much.

But it's not as simple as that.

Much as I'd like it to, feeling grateful for Gracie doesn't make things better. Because it's not designed to. One child is never meant to compensate for another.

My grief made Gracie feel unwanted. Unloved. Not enough.

But this is the point.

It's not that Gracie isn't enough, it's that she was never meant to be enough. She was meant to be one of two sisters.

She was meant to be herself, not herself plus a compensation for a lost sister.

I love Gracie more deeply than ever and I feel grateful for her and she's enough *in herself.*

I want to free her from the burden of thinking that she somehow needs to stand in for Molly. Life's hard enough just being Gracie in all the beauty and complexity and challenge of that. And I want her to focus on that, on being fully herself, not on making things better for me.

I want her to know that she can't take away my grief. Or make up for Molly being gone.

I want her to know that is not her job. And that remembering Molly and talking about Molly and sharing Molly's story with the world isn't about diminishing how much she means to me. It's about the fact that nothing can ever make up for having lost my child. The two things are separate.

~

Our relationship, after Molly died took on other levels of complexity. Beyond this battle of Gracie feeling like she somehow must suddenly be everything for me, both herself and Molly, was the pain of how completely our lives and our family had changed and how none of us knew how to navigate that landscape.

I'm no longer the same mother. Gracie is no longer the same daughter. Losing Molly changed both of us.

Quite a bit has been written about child loss. Comparatively little about sibling loss.

What people don't think about is that when a sibling loses a brother or sister, they lose much more too; they lose their parent or parents, who will never be the same again. They lose the family life they once had. Kenny, Gracie, and I can never re-create the dynamic that we had when Molly was here. Molly was too integral to how we were as a family for that. And

Gracie will never be the person she was when Molly was her sister, alive, standing, dancing, and sleeping next to her.

Gracie no longer has Molly.

And her family no longer exists, or not in the way it did.

The journey of grief I share with Gracie is one of the hardest things about this process. Perhaps harder even than dealing with all those people who want me to be done with grief already, those who don't understand.

You'd think that Molly's death would have brought us closer but, in truth, it's created a dynamic between us that I sometimes find impossible to navigate.

I feel as though Gracie can never understand the extent of what I've lost as a mother.

Gracie feels that I can never understand the extent of what she's lost as a sister.

And Gracie feels more than this too. Because when Molly died, she didn't just lose her sister, she lost her parents, her family, and her whole way of life as she knew it.

Kenny and I are broken people now. We are doing the best we can. Some days are better than others. But we'll never again be the mom and dad or the couple or the individuals we were when Molly was still alive. And Gracie feels it. She knows that she's lost who we used to be for her.

Gracie and I needed each other so badly, we needed help and comfort, but each of us was too wrapped up in our own grief to be able to give that.

Some days, when I'd cry and cry, saying, "Please come back, Molly, please come back," Gracie would snap back at me: "She's not coming back. Stop it."

My grief made her uncomfortable. It was too much. And it sometimes felt like a competition too. Which of us felt worse because Molly had died.? It made us intolerant of each other. And angry.

This is why, so often, families fall apart when a child dies. Everyone wants the other person to be what they need. Gracie wanted her mother, the mother who was strong and together and had the answers and knew what to do next, to make it all better for her. But Gracie's mother died when Molly died.

And I wanted the old Gracie back, my sweet happy girl who stood in the doorway of my bedroom, showing me Molly's pink dress, her eyes full of light and love for her sister and hope. But that Gracie died with her sister.

And we both wanted Kenny back, the dad who stood fixing the fence with Molly a few days before she died and gave them their baths as babies and laughed with them and played with them. But that Kenny died with Molly too.

We hadn't just lost Molly, we'd lost each other too.

Grief turns us inward. We do all we can simply to survive. We're no longer who we were, and we have little left to give even to those we love most.

Many of my arguments with Kenny were about our grief too. And our inability to be there for each other. I remember early on, I would sit on the couch and cry and cry and he would just sit there. He wouldn't even try to comfort me. He felt too lost. And too angry. Angry at the world for having taken Molly. But angry at me, too, in the way that parents are always angry at each other when their child gets sick or dies because the expectation is that somehow, we should have saved them.

In those early days, it was like we were sitting in the aftermath of a loud explosion or the collapse of a building. Our eyes and lungs and mouths were filled with dust and smoke. Our ears still rang from the sound of the explosion. We hardly knew whether we were alive or dead. How could we be there for each other when we couldn't even see each other anymore for all the smoke? Or hear each other's voices from the ringing in our ears? How could we be there for each other when we hardly knew if we ourselves were alive or dead?

Not that I didn't try to be there for Gracie. I knew I was her mother. I knew I needed to help her and support her. And if I'm kind to myself, I think I did my best. But it wasn't enough.

~

Gracie was angry with me in the same way that Kenny was angry with me. I was the mom. I was meant to save her sister. I'd failed at the one important job the universe had given me: keeping her little sister alive.

Gracie was a tender soul, to begin with, so her withdrawal inside herself when Molly died was who she was anyway. So, she kept to herself. She didn't go out much. She canceled plans with friends. School and dance and socializing were often too much for her. Grief is a full-time job. It doesn't leave much energy for normal living.

But over time, I began to sense a new strength in her, one that I'd first seen when she stood up to the nurse who said that we had to unplug Molly on the Friday. I'd seen it, too, when she took her friends, one by one, into Molly's hospital room to say goodbye. And I saw it the first recital after Molly died, when the T-shirts for the dance academy didn't have Molly's name on the list of dancers. I've never heard her scream so loud. She was so angry. Molly had danced at the dance academy since she was two years old and now, to Gracie, it felt like she was already forgotten.

The new Gracie spoke up. She advocated for herself. And for Molly. Molly's name was never left off that shirt again.

Molly's death changed Gracie. The grief changed her. But she was also growing up. When Molly died, Gracie was fifteen. Now, she's an adult. Old enough to have a baby of her own. Molly's death came at just the point where she was tilting on her own developmental axis, so things were shifting anyway. But I do think that this new strength came from Molly's death. If you've walked through fire and come out the other side alive, even if you're burned and limping and choking on smoke, a part of you knows that you can do anything now.

I heard the psychologist, Adam Grant, talking about the

difference between PTSD (post-traumatic stress disorder) and PTG (post-traumatic growth). We've heard lots about the former. The stress and anxiety and overwhelmingness that is the legacy of trauma. Gracie, Kenny, and I all had that. I think that anyone who loved and lost Molly so suddenly had that. But there's another kind of response to trauma that's less talked about. A more hopeful form. And I see it in Gracie. It's called post-traumatic growth. Parts of her will always feel weak and vulnerable and exposed because of losing Molly and losing her in the way she did. But I also see new, strong shoots of growth, shoots that say, "Look at what happened to me. But I'm still here. Don't underestimate me. And don't think that I will ever let anyone silence me in the way that my sister was silenced when she spoke up about her needs or her pain."

Or that's my hope for her. Because I'm her mother. Because I must believe that something good must come from all this. And because I believe, more profoundly than that, that Molly hasn't abandoned us. That her form and presence is different, but she is standing right by her sister in ways that we will never see or know or understand but which are helping Gracie turn into the strong, resilient young woman that she was always meant to be, stronger even, perhaps, because of what she lost.

Chapter 32
My Perfect Island

It's strange that, in the weeks after Molly's death, I often felt closer to complete strangers than I did to my friends and family.

I lived on Facebook. I know how people feel about social media. That it can be a cruel and damaging place, a place that can do more harm than good. But for me, it was a lifeline.

People messaged me constantly about Molly. It helped me feel connected and cared for and understood. And it felt like Molly's memory was being kept alive too. People weren't forgetting about her.

And then a few people mentioned some online grief groups they were part of what helped them when they lost a child. Those groups turned out to be one of the most important parts of my grief journey. I'm not sure how I could have survived without them.

Here, at last, were people—mothers, mostly, but a few fathers too—who understood. All the sympathy and empathy in the world from family and friends can't get to this place of understanding what it's really like to lose a child.

The first group I found is called Compassionate Friends. It's one of the oldest support groups out there.

I joined a few others. Ellie's Way was especially important to me, but I think I was part of fifteen or so groups in all. I was hungry to find people who saw me and what I'd been through. And to learn from those who were trying to live after the worst thing that life can throw at you had happened.

Certain families and children stood out to me and have become friends. And more than that, I've grown to love the lost children. I see them as having a kinship with Molly. I have their faces on my fridge, on Christmas ornaments, on coffee mugs. Most of us have set up foundations to raise money for good causes, an attempt to make something good come from our loss. We sell bracelets and T-shirts and stickers. And we support each other.

Vinnie died in March 2013. He was a high school senior. His brother had already graduated, and they were driving home from an awards ceremony at their school. They had an argument and Vinnie got out of the car and decided to walk home. On his walk home, he got hit by a car and died.

This was three years before Molly's death, so Vinnie's dad, E. R., who was in the group, was someone I looked to as having gotten through days and months and years without his son. I needed to see what it was like to survive. To go through the depths of grief and somehow come out the other side and try to make something positive of life, knowing that the pain and the loss will always be there.

The next person I met online was a little girl, Molly's age, called Marilee. She lived in Missouri. Her story was similar to Molly's. She was the same age. She'd had terrible headaches. But unlike Molly, she never had the opportunity for life support. One day she was there, an aneurysm burst, and then she was gone. Marilee, like Molly, had sought medical help prior to the rupture. Perhaps if she had been given a scan, they could have saved her.

Marilee's mother, Lisa, read my posts and the story of my lawsuit with keen interest. She asked me questions about everything that had happened during and after Molly's death. And I realized that in some ways, I'd had it easier than her.

I'd had a fight to channel my grief into, a lawsuit to occupy our time and our minds and to distract us from our sadness. Someone to be angry at besides myself.

Both Vinnie and Marilee had been known for their kindness as kids, a quality which doesn't come as easily to children as we might think. I remember saying to myself, "Why can't it be the shitty kids who die?" Which is awful and wrong. No child deserves to die. And no child is shitty, they're still growing into themselves and learning how to be in the world and much of their behavior is conditioned by their circumstances. But still, I had the thought because we do when these amazing kids die. Kids who are loved, kids who are known for their goodness and kindness and for the light they bring to their worlds. Kids like Vinnie, Marilee, and my Molly.

And then there was Jack. He died in August 2016 a few months after Molly. I saw his mom's name and her story pop up on Facebook late that summer. And it hit me: this is still happening. All over the world, every day, every second of every day, children are dying. For me, when Molly died, it felt like the world stopped, like nothing worse could ever happen. But the truth is that there are over 7 billion people living on the planet, 2.2 billion of those are children. And every year, over 10 million of those children die. UNICEF recently released the statistic that a child under the age of fifteen dies every five seconds. Not that this horrifying statistic lands with us, statistics rarely do. It's the individual stories that matter and our connection to them. Which is why I'm writing this book, not because my Molly's death was any more tragic than any of those other 10 million deaths that happened in 2016 but because one individual story sheds light and makes sense—and sensitizes us—to the whole.

And it's why these grief groups and these dead children I came to learn about and their grieving parents mean so much to me. They are real, individual stories that I can see and feel and learn about, that are made real to me and that help me feel less alone, which, when all is said and done, is the purpose of all good stories and all good human connections.

So, when I learned about Jack, it really hit home. This will keep happening. Children will keep dying. And this is my world now, my community, my island. And strange as it might sound, talking to those other grieving parents was the very first time I felt relief. I understood that no matter how kind or well-meaning or sympathetic people were, only they could understand the hell of living with child loss. I wanted to be with them. To share our feelings and our truths and our struggles. During that first summer and in the months and years that followed, if I could have designed a perfect island, it would have had me and those grieving parents on it and no one else. It was only with them that I felt seen and heard and understood, that I could breathe. People I would never have to explain myself to because they just knew.

Jack was thirteen too, like Molly and Marilee.

His mother had left him and his sister, Lily, with their grandparents and while they were there, Jack went to play in the woods with his friends. One of them had a firearm and it went off; Jack was shot in the neck. The children involved were so scared that they ran away and didn't tell anyone about Jack being injured until it was too late. He bled to death on his own in the woods. If he'd had medical attention earlier, he might still be alive today.

Sometimes it's people's stories I'm drawn to, or a connection to a parent and the way they grieve that resonates and speaks to me. For some reason, it was Jack's picture that made me sit up and take notice. He was thirteen when he died. But he still looked like a little boy. A beautiful boy with a sweet, open expression. A little boy who, like my Molly, should never have died.

Brandy, Jack's mother, and I connected immediately, and she was drawn to the pictures of Molly that I posted too. I think we both suspected that, in a different world, they would have been friends. Perhaps they are now.

Over the years, Jack and his name would come to hold a very, very special place in our new, Molly-less family.

I spent as much time as I could online with these families. We messaged each other in the middle of the night and at special moments that were hard for us. We might never meet, but we are there for each other in a profound way.

Being part of these groups helped, and I would encourage anyone who has lost a child—or who has lost anyone—even those of you who aren't so keen on online connections, to find a grief group that suits you. The online nature helps those of us who are grieving. Oftentimes you just don't feel like getting out of bed or having a shower or getting in a car or being sociable and forming part of an in-person group. Doing all those things can be helpful. But more times than not, you just want to be able to reach out, no matter what state you're in, no matter what time of the day or night it is, and to feel connected to someone who understands. These Facebook groups did that for me.

And then another Molly died at twenty-nine. Her mother, Cathy, was connected to me through a colleague of mine who was her Molly's cousin. I have a mug with her Molly on it and she has a MollyB hoodie. These connections came to mean so much to me.

There were people in my community too. People I knew or would come to know. When Molly died, Jon, a local friend, reached out to me. I remembered when his son, Nat, died by suicide sitting in front of a train. The story haunted me, and I'd reached out to him to express my sympathy. Looking back now, with a dead child of my own, I realize how inadequate my words were. I wasn't to blame for not finding the right words, just like those around me who haven't lost children who try to comfort me aren't to blame when their words fail, they just can't understand. Which is OK. Which is a good thing. The fewer people who experience, and so can empathize with, child loss, the better. But Jon and others who had lost children around me were now part of my club. My island. I got them in a whole new way. And I saw them cropping up everywhere. A bit like when you get pregnant for the first time and see big bellies everywhere or when you buy an orange car and suddenly there are orange cars all over the highway. Parents who had experienced child loss began to cross my path.

When I went to Molly's grave at Blossom Hill Cemetery one day, I met two mothers who had lost their sons. They became friends when their children died. We shared our stories. I told them about Molly. After that, they told me that they always stopped by Molly's grave to say hello and to send up a prayer. I would go to their sons' graves too, to leave flowers.

As people, we couldn't have been more different. They were bikers, part of those hard-drinking, hard-partying New Hampshire people whom I typically wouldn't have crossed paths with. But we were part of the same island now. We were more than friends. When we saw each other in town, we stopped to hug each other without even needing to say a word.

No one should ever have to lose a child; it's the most cruel and unnatural of things. But there are situations that arise from losing a child that deepen your humanity. Recognizing the superficial barriers that separate us from others, the barriers that can be torn down in an instant with a shared experience like child loss, has given me a much deeper connection to everyone in the world. It has made me more open and compassionate and accepting. My island, though small in its membership and exclusive in its requirement —you need to have a dead child— is in every other way the most inclusive island in the world.

Chapter 33

Be the Miracle

Finally, and perhaps most powerfully for us as a family, there was Rachel, who died three years after Molly. Her family came to join us on our island of grief. And to me, they were another sign of how everything is connected. Of those thousand tiny steps that join everything like one of those dot-to-dot pictures children love to draw. Rachel was the blonde girl with the long legs, the high school senior who'd danced in the opening number of *MollyB the Musical*. And she was the girl who ended up giving her kidney to Kenny.

On a warm day in April 2019, when I was sitting outside in a lawn chair with my computer, I saw a message come up on the dance academy Facebook page. One of their dancers was on life support at the same children's hospital where Molly had spent the last week of her life.

The hairs on the back of my neck stood up.

Not again, I remember thinking. *Not again.*

I called up Cindy, the owner of the dance academy who had walked with us in our grief, who had taught Molly to dance, to ask what was going on and I could hear the relief in her voice, "Oh, thank God. This family really needs you," Cindy said. "Please reach out to them."

We didn't know Rachel's family well. The ages of our girls didn't quite line up. But they were a dance family, and our girls danced in the big musical numbers together: *The Jersey Boys* one year, *It's a Musical* another year, and we recognized Allie's and Rachel's names from the show programs. But beyond that, our paths hadn't really crossed much. We didn't know, then, that we were about to become part of each other's island.

When Rachel got sick, none of that mattered. I knew that this family was going through the worst experience of their lives; they had a sick child, on life support. And Cindy was right, they needed us. Not because we were special but because we'd been there. We understood.

As soon as I got off the phone, I sent Jennifer a Facebook message:

"You don't know me. I'm Barb Higgins, Molly's mom. We've been where you are. Regardless of what happens to Rachel, your life is going to be very different. You're going to need support. Would it be OK for me to set up a GoFundMe account for you and organize some meals?"

"Oh, OK. Yes. That would be fine," Jenn said, her voice far away.

I could tell that she didn't know what was happening or what they would need as a family. She was in survival mode. I'd been there too.

I pushed the campaign on social media and, explaining what had happened to Rachel and how much this family needed our support, soon raised $25,000 for the Hungers. When Molly was in the hospital, our friends and family raised close to $30,000. That money helped us to survive at a time when we were already in financial difficulty as a family.

We designed T-shirts saying "Be the Miracle" to raise more money and support for them.

Rachel had a tattoo on her arm, inspired by her grandmother who died the year before. It said, "Born to be the Miracle."

It was Rachel's life mantra. That to be the miracle in someone's life, you didn't have to do the big things, to make grand, dramatic gestures. You could make a huge difference, you could bring about a miracle through the smallest acts of kindness.

She gave blood regularly. That was one of her ways of being the miracle.

She was like Molly in that way. She saw it as her purpose to make life better for others.

Through it all, we hoped that Rachel might still wake up. That her story would have a different ending from Molly's.

Kenny and I drove straight up to the hospital along with Cindy and one of her dance teachers, Hillary. As soon as Jenn saw me, she walked right past Cindy and Hillary, whom she knew, and came up to me, whom she didn't know, and gave me the biggest hug. She already knew that we were on the same island. That I understood.

We went to Rachel's room and the minute Kenny and I saw her, we knew. When you've seen your child who's never going to wake up plugged into machines, you know what that looks like. It was all so familiar. And it was clear to us at that moment that, like Molly, Rachel would never wake up. I hate that we were right. I took Rachel's hand in mine.

I thought back to the times I'd slept with Molly in her narrow hospital bed when she was on life support. How the nurses told me to then, too, that when I was close, all of Molly's numbers settled. How she was calm. I wanted the same for Rachel. As I stroked her hand, her numbers settled.

I knew it already, but those moments confirmed to me that even when a person is unconscious, even when we feel like they're a million miles away from us, like they can't hear or see us, like they're dead inside their bodies, their spirit feels our touch and our love. It responds to us.

Gradually, I learned what had happened to Rachel. That she'd been to a restaurant and ordered egg rolls, the same kind she'd had before. And gone into anaphylactic shock.

Rachel has lived with allergies her whole life. She's allergic to a bunch of things, but the worst is her peanut allergy. She always carried two EpiPens with her. She read the ingredients list of everything she put in her mouth. The problem was that no one told her there was peanut paste in the egg roll that day.

She started having a severe reaction as she left the restaurant.

She used her EpiPens right away, but they didn't make a difference.

Then she went back to her apartment with her friend and called her mom.

"I'm scared," she said.

"You don't need to be scared," her mom said. "You're going to be OK."

Words that would come to haunt Jenn.

"OK, I have to go," Rachel said. "I can hear the sirens. They're here."

When her EpiPens failed to make a difference, Rachel had called 911.

Jenn tells me that when she heard that the ambulance was there, she felt relieved, like we all feel relieved as if by a primal reflex when our kid is sick and the doctor shows up. *She's in safe hands now,* Jenn told herself.

But during that ambulance ride, a ride that was far too slow considering the severity of Rachel's symptoms, she went into cardiac arrest, and her brain was starved of oxygen for almost thirty minutes. She slipped into a coma, and she never woke up.

The family has been fighting to get Rachel's Law passed. A law that would oblige all restaurants to train their staff in greater awareness of food allergies and to create better labeling. Rachel should have been told that the egg roll was stuck together with peanut paste. She would never have ordered it. She would have lived.

Deciding to unplug Rachel was hugely difficult for her parents. The doctors said that her brain had been starved of so much oxygen that even if she did wake up, she wouldn't have any cognitive function left. But I understood, it never feels right to take your child off the machines that are keeping her body alive. Even if all hope is lost, you still want to believe that there will be a miracle.

So, I sat with Rachel and held her hand and spoke to her. I told her that everything was going to be OK. That she could let go. That I believed that she and Molly would find each other and do amazing things. That I would take care of her mom and that Kenny would take care of her dad and that Gracie would be there for her siblings, especially her sister, Allie. That we would help them through their grief. That if this was her time, she should feel at peace.

Then I went back to the waiting room.

Jenn came in and hugged me.

And she asked me about organ donation and what I'd decided to do with Molly. Sadness swept over me again.

"We didn't get to give Molly's organs because we didn't know whether her tumor was cancerous. Instead, we had to bury her with her perfect body and her healthy organs. We were so sad," I told her. "We thought that maybe Kenny could have gotten Molly's kidney. It would have been a beautiful thing, to have part of her living inside her father, saving him. But that never happened."

Jennifer looked surprised. "Kenny needs a kidney?"

I nodded. "He's on dialysis. He's got kidney disease. His kidney is failing. And we don't have a donor."

Molly had died, not Kenny. But the horrible truth was that Kenny could still die. He was still really sick.

"What's his blood type?" Jenn asked.

"O positive."

Jenn's eyes widened. "That's Rachel's blood type."

We both went quiet. A knowingness was exchanged between us. But we didn't articulate what we were feeling. Perhaps we needed time to process it, to acknowledge the enormity of this thread that was connecting us. Our dead daughters. Their bodies. The gifts we would give each other through our grief.

It was five days later, we were at the cemetery, commemorating the third year since Molly's death, when Jenn called us to ask for Kenny's transplant coordinator details. It was the day of Rachel's twenty-first birthday.

The next day, May 8, the day Rachel was unplugged, Kenny went to Mass. General Hospital and got a kidney transplant.

Kenny got Rachel's kidney.

I like to say that the kidney that danced at Molly's memorial, at the musical that celebrated her life and honored her death, now lives in Molly's dad. Tell me that life isn't connected by a million invisible threads. Tell me that there aren't a thousand tiny steps between each moment and each living thing on our earth. I need to write that again:

Kenny got Rachel's kidney.

Rachel was the miracle in our lives like she'd been the miracle in the lives of so many people she knew when she was alive. She saved Kenny's life.

In the days and weeks that followed, we supported Rachel's family in every way we could. All the exhausting practicalities of dealing with the death of a child. We gave them the name of our funeral home, we told them to get a headstone. I called ahead to prepare the people there for the Hungers. And we gave all the emotional support we could too. Because now we shared an island. We knew what it was like to live in a new world where no one else could understand the enormity of our grief except those who had felt that grief in their own lives. How it made you feel like an alien. An outsider. Someone who no longer belonged or played by the same rules. A world where you lose a child and must keep getting up morning after morning to face a new day. A world that, often, you wished you no longer had to live in anymore.

On days when Kenny and I are having a hard time, Gracie goes to stay with Rachel's family. She now works at Little Sprouts in Bow, Jenn's day-care center.

On days when Allie, Rachel's younger sister, is having a

hard time, she comes over to stay with us.

Even when we don't see each other for a while, we're there for each other. We don't need to explain. And when things get hard, we have a support system in place.

Most of all, Ally and Gracie have become like sisters to each other. I would do anything in my power to bring Rachel back to life for her family, but Ally's friendship has saved Gracie. She has one person whom she knows who understands. I have found them at the cemetery together, sitting on Molly's grave or a bit higher up at Rachel's grave. The four sisters hanging out. The living and the dead. I like to think of Molly and Rachel together, wherever they are, looking down at us as we muddle through our lives without them. I hope they have each other. I hope that they're dancing together. I hope that it's easier over there than it is over here.

The donation of Rachel's kidney gave Gracie her dad back too. The kidney transplant went better than the doctors had expected. Kenny is strong and healthy again. He got a second chance. We all did.

I struggle with the *it-happens-for-a-reason* mantra. There doesn't seem to be a single reason in the world to justify a child dying. But I do believe that woven through these inexplicable, unjustifiable tragedies, miracles happen. Like the Hungers giving Kenny Rachel's kidney so that he could live. That there are a thousand tiny steps that connect every moment, every decision with every living thing. That it's like a country. A kind of Motherland.

Chapter 34
The Dreams

There was another dimension to grief and to losing Molly that was particular to me.

In that last week of her death, I had my period. Molly did too. It broke my heart, thinking that the beginning of my thirteen-year-old's reproductive journey was taking place on her deathbed. That she'd never get to be a mother. To make life.

It turns out that at the very same time, my reproductive journey was ending. This would be my last period. Perhaps it was the shock of Molly's death that sent me into menopause or maybe it was coming anyway, but as the summer after Molly's death wore on, as I went through May and June in a fog of grief, I suddenly got to mid-July and realized that my period had never come back.

In the week that Molly was in the hospital, she had her last period. So did I. She was thirteen. I was fifty-two.

In the weeks and months after her death, the symptoms of menopause set in. I would wake up on my living room floor bed with beads of sweat covering my body. I remember thinking: *so, this is the end of the road for me. I don't get to be a mother again.*

I'd been thinking about that in the lead-up to Gracie's fifteenth birthday. I told myself that in a few years, she'd be a college senior and then she'd be off. All grown up. No longer in need of a mother. I know, deep down, that being a mother never ends, that your child can be a parent or even a grandparent themselves and that you're still their mom. But it's not the same, is it? While they're still living under your roof and going to school and sleeping in their childhood bedrooms and expecting you to pay the grocery bill and organize their doctors' visits, when their skin still reminds you of their baby skin, then your mothering is more primal and essential. And I knew that as Gracie was growing up that was coming to an end, and I wasn't quite sure how I'd handle that.

But I told myself, it would be OK. I'd have another two years of mothering Molly. She'd still be here. She'd still need me.

But now she was gone.

My mothering, already with a clear expiration date, had suddenly and unexpectedly been cut short by two years. Or that's how it felt.

The coming together of Molly's death and my menopause screamed at me loud and clear: your mothering days are over. A thought that's hard for any mother to stomach, even those with living children going out into the world, but for me, it was devastating.

I went into a tailspin of panic.

And that's when the dreams came.

~

Dreams can take on all sorts of shapes.

At first, my dreams weren't visual. I didn't remember them like a film reel playing behind my eyes. But when I woke up, I had a clear message and a clear feeling: I was meant to have a baby.

It was the summer after Molly's death. I hadn't fallen back into drugs then, so the dreams were real, they weren't my broken mind playing games with me. I felt that they were telling me something. Something I need to pay attention to.

Mornings were hard for me. I slept and as soon as I woke up, I'd get up. I couldn't stand lying down with my thoughts. I knew that would undo me. So, as soon as my eyes opened, I sprung up, made myself a coffee, and sat on the porch and tried to find a way to get through another day without Molly.

But the first time I woke up from that baby dream, I couldn't get up right away. The feelings were too powerful. I lay there paralyzed by the thought that my grieving heart and mind couldn't yet make sense of, that I was somehow meant to have a baby.

Later that July, I was due to have a checkup with my OB-GYN. I was having a bad day. I couldn't stop crying. I felt like the world was falling out from under me. I thought about canceling but I knew I had to take care of myself, if not for me then for Gracie. I had to keep doing these things that normal people do.

I had the appointment with a nurse practitioner. It was routine. And then at the end, in my shaky voice, I told her about the dream. And how I felt. That I thought that I was somehow meant to have a baby.

I remember the look of horror and disgust that crossed her face. And then she said, "No! You need to get that thought out of your head now. That would not be a good idea at all. That would be very, very dangerous."

I'd done my research. I knew that medically it was possible for doctors to give me hormones that would restart my periods, to pull me out of menopause. That through IVF, I could have another baby. But this nurse wasn't telling me I *couldn't* have a baby, she was telling me that I didn't have a right to.

Her response was so firm and negative that it took me aback.

"Oh ... OK. Thank you," I said.

I stumbled out of her office stunned, paid my bill and knew, in that moment, that I would never go back there.

And then it hit me. I wasn't crazy. Or wrong to ask for this. A woman coming to a medical professional, being vulnerable, sharing her thoughts and her pain, asking for help should never be shut down.

My first reaction was to feel hurt but also be deferential. She was a medical professional. She knew what she was talking about. She was right, it was stupid of me to even think of having a baby. I'm old. I'm grieving. That's all there is to it. I should just move on.

I bowed to her judgment. To her medical knowledge and expertise. You'd have thought that I'd have been better able to stand up for myself, but at that time, I was broken and grieving and scared and I doubted everything about myself and my life and my decisions. And the conditioning ran deep. I'd grown up in a world that trusted the medical professional like we trust God. They know best.

When I spoke up, I was made to feel like I was foolish or damaged or dangerous or deranged, probably a mix of all those things. I was made to feel like I shouldn't trust my own thoughts or my own dreams or my own body. It's been happening for thousands of years. It's probably how the witch hunts started. Women with dangerous ideas and strong feelings that threaten the status quo need to be shut down.

That nurse practitioner might not have known it, she might have thought she was genuinely protecting *me* from danger, but what she was saying was clear: to even entertain the thought of having a baby at fifty-two was dangerous, not for me (many women have had babies in their fifties) but dangerous for the world. Because who knows what will happen if we listen to women's feelings, to their pain, to their ideas and longings and dreams—really listen—and then act on it? The whole world order would fall apart.

Imagine what a dangerous message it would send out to our neat, ordered, patriarchal, civilized society if women started giving birth when they had wrinkles on their faces, when they were half a century old? Oh, when men father children in their eighties, they're considered virile. Clapped on the back. Looked at with admiration. But an old mother, an old woman having a baby, that's dangerous and disgusting.

And the terrible thing was that it was a woman who'd made me feel like that.

But the thing about dreams, and the subconscious, is that it doesn't pay much attention to medical professionals or to patriarchal judgments. It keeps working its way regardless. And so, the baby dreams kept coming.

It took me a long time to tell Kenny. I thought he might react badly, so I kept my dreams to myself for a while. But when, eventually, I sat with him in the early morning on the porch, drinking coffee, like we did every morning since Molly died, he didn't even blink. He was on board. Neither of us understood how it would work or what it would look like, but he was in.

That's one of the remarkable things about Kenny. When it comes to being a father, to having a baby, he's not fazed. For him, it's the most natural thing in the world. I love him for that. That he heard me and saw me and just went with it, no questions asked because he believed that what I was saying was real and true. That I wasn't just a grieving lunatic.

As the summer wore on, the drive to have a child got stronger. It was my first thought when I woke up in the morning. One minute I'd be sound asleep and the next I'd be sitting up with a voice in my head that wouldn't be silenced: *I have to have a baby! I have to have a baby!*

And I tried to silence it. I told myself that I was panicking because of having lost Molly and that I was sad that my mothering years were cut short. That I was menopausal. That these thoughts probably came to women the world over as they faced the reality that they wouldn't have a baby again.

But the thoughts and the dreams kept coming.

And then, in the beginning of fall 2016, I had my first vivid, visual dream, and there was no going back from there.

~

In the dream, I was driving along a dark country road with a bunch of moms whose daughters danced with Molly and Gracie. We were driving fast, and the roads were curvy. And then, suddenly, we were standing on a farmhouse porch and one of the moms handed me a vial and said, "Drink this if you want to have a baby."

Not long after that dream, I was driving home from an early-morning cross-country practice. I drove past the middle school where Molly would have started up eighth grade if she hadn't died. It was unbearable looking at those school doors. And then a voice boomed out at me, so loud my head hurt:

"Barbara! Barbara!" it yelled. "Call about the baby!

I pulled off to the side of the road and made an appointment with an OB-GYN doctor at Dartmouth Hitchcock, Dr. Chaudhari. His first available appointment was October 16, weeks away. I asked to be put on the cancelation list. I said I'd come at the drop of a hat. But there were no cancelations, so I waited.

And when, eventually, I went into his office, I was worried that I'd be told, again, that I was foolish and dangerous and that I should forget it. But that's not what happened.

Dr. Chaudhari was wonderful. He told me about a fifty-two-year-old woman whom he'd taken to full term and who now had a beautiful baby. I was fifty-three. I could do it too. After some blood work, he assessed that with the stage I'd reached in my menopause and with the complication of Kenny's vasectomy, we wouldn't be able to conceive naturally, but through IVF we had a good chance. We could do this, he said. He gave me hope. He believed in me.

At first, I was a bit sad that I couldn't do it all myself. That I would need significant hormonal assistance. But I soon learned—and I continue to learn now—that there's no going back to that time. That things are different now. That we would need all the help we could get to make this baby. And that that was OK.

All I had to do was find an IVF clinic that would take me. I was now fifty-three years old.

I had told my friend Polly about my dreams. She's one of those friends you can tell anything to, and she'll go along with it. I could ask her to rob a bank with me tomorrow and she'd be on board. So, I knew that I could trust her with this, my longing to have a baby.

She gave me the number of a doctor she knew who dealt with older women. She, in turn, referred me to Cardone Reproductive Medicine and Infertility, a clinic near Boston that included women in their fifties. There I met Dr. Vito Cardone. It wasn't lost on me that he was Italian, a culture that celebrates women and children and the whole process of giving life.

From the moment I met him, I knew that we'd get along. He was near retirement but still full of life and humor and his love for what he did was obvious. There was also no judgment. It didn't matter how old I was; if I was healthy and I passed all the medical tests needed to make sure that I was in a fit state to carry and deliver a baby, then he was on board.

In the next few months, I took all the first steps toward trying for a baby. Blood tests. A mammogram, a colonoscopy. A hysteroscopy that looked at the tissue in my uterus to see if it could make a baby. I passed everything with flying colors. In January 2017, we drove to Boston and talked through the process to have a baby through IVF. And then we were told how much it would cost.

I should have known that IVF wouldn't be cheap. That at our age and stage in life, we would have to have even more expensive treatments than a young couple going through the process. But I suppose I'd wanted to push it as far as it would go. When we were told that it would cost over $30,000, we knew we couldn't do it. I wasn't working much and Kenny wasn't working at all because of his kidney. We were barely making ends meet. There was no way we could afford this.

As we drove back from the clinic, we both felt overwhelmingly sad. I remember looking out the car window at the sky thinking:

No more dreams. I've done my best. I've taken this as far as it will go. I've pushed on every door. If something happens to change this, to make it possible, I'll do it. But right now, there's nothing more I can give.

And that's where it ended, for a while.

We got into the thick of the legal battle. I was pulled into taking drugs again to numb the pain and to avoid having to face the reality of my new Molly-less life.

And then the case ended, and, with it, the dreams came back too. On one of our regular mornings on the porch, drinking coffee, trying to make sense of our new lives without Molly, I turned to Kenny and said, "Guess what dream I had last night?"

He smiled. "The baby dream?"

I nodded.

I've come to believe that when you really want something and if that something is hard or unusual or goes against the grain of how the world does things, you'll be thrown a few obstacles along the way to test your mettle. I've had enough obstacles in my life to know that you just dust yourself off and begin again. The athlete in me was well trained in this process too. A setback isn't defeat, it's just a sign that you need to train harder.

So, we went back to Dr. Cardone.

Kenny and I got healthy. I swore to myself that I wouldn't take drugs again; this mattered more. Life mattered more.

That's why I think Molly might have had a hand in this. Over and over, I begged her to come to me. To give me signs that she could hear and see me. That even though her physical body was no longer here, that her spirit hadn't left me. I asked her to come to me in my dreams because it was at nighttime that I felt most lost and lonely.

And the dreams came. They weren't about Molly or in Molly's voice or an obvious communication from her. They were about having a baby. About being a mother again. About bringing new life into the world. So, how could they not, in some way, have been from her?

Having the baby also saved my life. In order to proceed, I had to stop taking my medication, and I was taking a lot. I had medication for depression and anxiety. For panic and insomnia. I also had medication for my mouth. I treated a long-time nerve condition with anti-seizure medication. None of these pills can be taken while pregnant. It took me three months to wean off all those pills.

During this time, my mouth began to hurt. I knew fairly quickly that I would not be able to manage a nine-month pregnancy without the medicine. I had to fix the nerve. I found a surgeon who specialized in trigeminal neuralgia treatment. Although he was in New York City, he agreed to see me. I had an MRI to see if I qualified for the surgery. An hour after that MRI, I received a phone call. They had found three brain tumors. My excitement over fixing my mouth and making a baby was quickly replaced with fear. I was devastated. The whole time I was fighting for Molly, I had these tumors in my head. Perhaps if I had known, they would have listened to her. It terrified Gracie who already had a sick father and a dead sister. All she wanted was a normal senior year of high school. Once again, I was being tested with an obstacle that at times felt impossible to conquer. Dr. Eskandar was not only able to remove the tumors, he also fixed my nerve condition. He took care of me. I spent these six months taking care of my head rather than making a baby and while it was frustrating, it showed me, once again, that there are good doctors out there who listen to and work with their patients. Who take their words seriously. Who believe them. He would be required to approve my continuation with IVF.

If I hadn't had those dreams of having a baby, if I hadn't

fought to pursue those dreams, even though they felt strange and impossible, I would never have found my way out of the spiral of addiction, I would never have found the brain tumors, which could have killed me. I would never have found my way back to life.

Three months after my brain surgery, we passed all the medical tests and began the process. Conception in a lab, transfer in a clinic.

I knew almost right away that I wasn't pregnant. I waited and peed on the stick far too early but even then, my body knew it hadn't worked. I remember feeling somewhat detached and not as upset as I thought I would be. Maybe the reason for all of this was about saving my life and not necessarily being a mother once again.

When we went for our follow-up with Dr. Cardone, we could tell he was disappointed. It should have worked. It was not you, he said. You should be pregnant.

"Can we try again?" I asked him.

I remember him smiling. "Are you going to twist my arm?"

I smiled back. "Yes, if that's what it takes."

We re-did all the tests. And we did some different things this time.

Then COVID hit, and everything shut down and my dream of having a baby was put on hold once again.

The funny thing is that I wasn't terribly upset about all these delays. I felt an odd sense of calm that if this was meant to happen, if I was meant to be a mother again, then the universe would make it work. I believed that this was a path that I was meant to pursue. And I promised myself that I'd give it everything I had. But if it turned out not to work, even after overcoming all the obstacles thrown our way, then I'd make my peace with it.

The world ground to a halt. We stayed home. Gracie and I had to be extra careful with Kenny. He'd recently had his kidney transplant, so he was vulnerable. We feared that if he got

COVID, he wouldn't survive.

And then, in May 2020, I got a phone call from Dr. Cardone's assistant. They were ready to try again.

By July, I was pregnant.

This time I knew. Even when the line was so faint it could have been my imagination willing it to be on that pregnancy stick, I knew. There was a baby growing inside me. I was going to be a mother again.

Chapter 35
A Quiet Pregnancy

Unusually for me, I kept the pregnancy a secret, even from Gracie. I'd lost a baby before at twenty-six weeks. I knew that telling the world too early would be a mistake. And my pregnancy was high risk, since I was fifty-seven. That said, my OB-GYN, Dr. Chaudhari, often commented that I was fitter than most of his young patients. Throughout the pregnancy, I went to CrossFit and lifted weights that most twenty-year-olds would struggle with. I may have a few more wrinkles than the average pregnant woman, but in every other way my body was ready.

We didn't tell Gracie because we knew it would be an emotional minefield. Her journey of grief was different from mine. I knew that she felt that she'd lost her parents, or the parents she knew, as well as her sister. Her family would never be the same. Kenny and I were consumed with grief. We thought of Molly and her death every second of every day. We couldn't be there for her in the way we were before. She told me a few times that she felt like my obsession with keeping Molly's story alive and the extent of my grief was a sign that she wasn't enough for me. I understood where these feelings come from. But she was never meant to be enough. She was meant to be herself: Gracie, one of my two girls. No matter how wonderful she was or how hard she tried or how much we loved her, she couldn't make up for Molly's death. She wasn't Molly. In that sense, she wasn't enough. I knew that when she found out about the baby, she'd think that it was another way that I was trying to fill the hole in my life after Molly died and that she'd be hurt again. I was telling the world that having only Gracie wasn't enough. But the baby wasn't about that either. This baby wouldn't replace Molly. He or she would be a whole new and different person.

Anyway, we thought it was best not to tell Gracie until we were sure that this baby was here to stay.

As for the rest of the world, I didn't want my pregnancy to be their business, not yet. People would have strong opinions about me doing this. They would question my motivation for having a baby and would judge my age and its implications. Before the day I got to hold my baby in my arms, I didn't want this judgment. COVID helped. I was able to stay home with my growing belly. It was only in the final stages that I got some stares and comments, but those weren't as bad as I expected. Those who truly loved me, the real friends, were pleased for me.

And the pregnancy went well. I was monitored closely. We had lots of scans. Dr. Chaudhari was amazed at how healthy the baby and I were. As was the wider medical community with which he shared my files.

As a high school senior, I was the first woman in New Hampshire to run under a five-minute mile.

As a fifty-seven-year-old woman, I was the oldest mother in New Hampshire to have carried a baby to term, which was a landmark. The fact that I was so fit and healthy and had no complications made my pregnancy even more intriguing to the medical world.

I remember Dr. Chaudhari looking me in the eye at one point and saying, "You know that this is going to get a lot of attention, don't you Barb?"

I was used to attention. My life has felt like one drama after the next, all played out in the public arena.

"I know, I know, people will have strong opinions," I said.

"That's not what I mean. Your pregnancy is a game changer. You're telling women, well into their fifties, that they can deliver a healthy baby. That's huge. You're going to have to prepare yourself for a great deal of publicity."

I don't think it really sank in, the publicity part at least. But I remember feeling happy that I was doing something for women. It felt like part of the journey I've been on ever since Molly died, making sure that as many young girls and women as possible are seen and heard by the medical profession. Older women who want to have babies are often silenced and shunned like I was by that first OB-GYN nurse. It's time that changed. Dr. Chaudhari was telling me that the act of me getting pregnant and delivering a baby at fifty-seven would help counter the prejudice against older women and their reproductive rights. That felt good.

I watched my belly grow, my breasts swell, my body grow thicker as it retained water and shifted in the way that a female body does as it goes about building a life.

And then, a few weeks before Jack's due date, came the final obstacle. There had to be one. The pregnancy had been too easy.

Chapter 36

One Last Push

I should have learned by now, by the age of fifty-seven with a thousand experiences of having my plans turned on their heads, that I couldn't control when or how Jack was going to be born.

But still, I had my plan, and when it fell to pieces, I was angry. It's hard to learn these lessons.

On Thursday the eighteenth of March, I went for a routine protein test for my pregnancy. I was monitored more closely and given more treatments because of my age. My blood pressure was low. I was fine. Everything was going to plan. Jack's due date was the thirteenth of April. I still had some time to get ready for him to come into my world and into the world.

And then I went home, and my legs started to swell, and I felt off and by mid-afternoon when I went back to the hospital, my blood pressure had shot up and my blood platelets were worryingly low.

I knew that Dr. Chaudhari was going away this weekend. He'd planned to be away in late March, so that he was sure to be around for the birth. I wasn't ready to go through this without him. Whatever happened, this baby could wait until Monday, it was just a few days, then he'd be back.

On Friday morning, I went to have more blood work done. It was meant to take ten minutes; I was there for three hours.

A feisty doctor told me that she didn't want me to leave, that I needed to be monitored. But I wasn't ready to hear that. This wasn't the plan. I explained that I didn't have any of my things, that we only had one car, that there was so much I had to do at home. Gracie had a dance competition. Kenny wasn't ready. *I* wasn't ready to have this baby. I fought hard for her to release me. I told her I'd be fine. And I went home.

I ran around in a panic. I asked a photographer friend to take pictures of me with my bump. I cleaned up the house. I made phone calls. I started an interview with the *Patch*, a local paper that wanted to cover my story.

By the time I was back at the hospital, my blood pressure was 197 over 105. I realized that I had to stay there. They said that I had pre-eclampsia. I needed close monitoring.

I was angry and resistant, but I couldn't argue with facts. Something was wrong, and if I left the hospital again, I was putting my and Jack's lives in danger.

It wasn't the high blood pressure or the danger I was in that got to me most that weekend, it was being in the same hospital where Molly had died. Again and again, I had to tell myself that these were different doctors and nurses in a different department, that I could trust them and that, if for a second, I felt like I wasn't receiving the care I needed, I could advocate for myself. They still remembered what had happened to Molly. All I had to do was summon her name and they'd listen to me.

Over the years, I've sent several friends and family members into the hospital wearing MollyB T-shirts, knowing that they'd be taken more seriously when the doctors realized that they knew my daughter's story.

That night the nurse had to strip my membranes. I have a high pain threshold. I'm tough. But this was painful. As the doctor pounded my insides and the nurse pinned me down to the bed to keep me from thrashing around, I was reminded of that scene in *The Handmaid's Tale* where Offred is being raped by the father of the baby and the wife is holding her down. It was an absurd thought but something about there being three of us and in this most intimate of processes, the configuration, the pain, and the pinning down, it felt primitive and brutal. I had a doctor halfway up my vagina and a nurse holding me down.

"Do you watch *The Handmaid's Tale*?" I joked to the nurse.

She got the reference right away.

The doctor didn't know the book or the show but said, "I have the feeling I'm the bad guy here."

At 9:00 p.m., they inserted a tablet to thin out my cervix. They said they would give me Pitocin in the morning to start labor. They had to get the baby before my blood pressure got any higher.

~

When I woke up the next morning, the ward was quiet. I ordered a coffee and breakfast to be brought up from the cafeteria. It didn't feel like anything momentous would happen today. Just more tests and waiting. If they did induce labor, it would probably take a good twelve hours or more.

"How are you feeling?" the doctor asked when she came in.

"OK, I guess," I said.

"And the contractions, how are they?"

The words hit me. "Contractions? No. I'm not having any contractions. Not yet."

They hadn't even given me any Pitocin yet. I couldn't be in labor.

The doctor looked at me. "You've been having contractions since 3:00 a.m."

I'd felt some heat and some discomfort in my belly but nothing like the contractions I remembered from having Molly and Gracie.

"It looks like labor started shortly after we stripped your membranes and thinned your cervix," she said.

By 9:30 a.m., I could feel the contractions, they were coming fast and hard.

At 11:00 a.m., they broke my water. The contractions got even worse. I asked for an epidural. They called the team, put in the needle, but I felt no relief or numbness.

Kenny was there by now. He said that they were exchanging odd looks like they knew something we didn't. I thought that I was going to be in labor for hours.

And then another doctor, a younger one said, "Why don't we see if you're ready to push."

~

"Already?"

She nodded. I lay down, and she put her hand inside me and said, "I can feel his head, he's ready to come out."

We'd talked to them about how we were having a boy. A boy after two girls. How we'd wanted to know.

With the next wave of contractions, I gave a half-hearted push.

"He's right here!" the doctor said. "If you push harder next time, we can get his head."

I gave one strong, forceful push, and he came out, not just his head, but all of him. I remember how surprised everyone looked.

Jack was born at 12:31 p.m., four hours after I woke up that morning. We named him after Brandy's little boy, the boy who died from a gunshot wound in the woods three months after Molly died. It's my way of letting her know that her little boy and his life and his story will be remembered.

~

On Thursday, when I started getting symptoms of pre-eclampsia, I was angry. I wasn't ready for this to happen. Jack wasn't meant to be born yet. And I'd worked so hard to stay healthy, to make this pregnancy OK and now, at the last minute, it was all going wrong.

By Friday, I was resigned to the fact that I had to be in the hospital, that they had to monitor me and that he would probably be born that weekend without Dr. Chaudhari.

And by Saturday, my anger which had turned to resignation turned to resolve. I was going to have my little boy. It was all going to be OK.

And through all of it, surprisingly perhaps, I didn't feel scared. I was irritated and frustrated but not scared. Perhaps that's one of the small blessings for those of us who have been through and seen the worst. We are better prepared for what life can throw at us. We're not so scared anymore.

Looking back, the fact that he was born on the first day of spring, the twentieth of March, a holy day in the Bahá'í Faith that marks a new beginning, was perfect. As everything else, this played out how it was meant to.

Jack was tiny. They'd have to keep Jack and me in the hospital for a few days. But I was OK. And he was OK. We'd done this.

A rainbow baby is a child born after a child dies. Often through miscarriage. Gracie was a rainbow baby, coming after the death of Baby Gordy at twenty-six weeks. Baby Jack was a rainbow baby too; he came after his sister Molly died.

And so, with Kenny at my side, I delivered my fourth child. My second rainbow baby. And a new chapter of our lives began.

Chapter 37

The News Gets Out

As I lay in the hospital, holding my new baby, I braced myself for the world to judge me for having done this. I knew that many, like that first OB-GYN nurse I saw shortly after Molly's death, would tell me that I was foolish and that in choosing to have a baby so late, I'd done something wrong. Wrong for me. Wrong for the baby. And wrong for the world. I'd sent out a dangerous message: being an old mother was OK.

I understand their concerns. But I have some answers too.

Men father children into their eighties, and no one questions it. Sure, their biology is wired differently from ours, but still, the disparity in our responses to old fathers versus old mothers strikes me as part of a wider sexual inequality.

I've been told that I'll be a grandma when my son is in his teens. That it will be embarrassing for him to have such an old parent. That I'll probably be dead by the time he's in his twenties or thirties and that this will be hard on him.

Grandparents around the world have raised children in the most beautiful and loving ways. Often better than younger parents. When Kenny and I were parents the first time around, we were tied up with our jobs and earning money and our social lives and our personal ambitions and relationships and pursuits. We weren't nearly as available as we are now for Jack. The quality of parenting Jack will have from us in his early years will, I'd argue, be superior to the many millions of children who spend their childhood in day care or being passed around babysitters.

As for the getting old and dying thing, well, if Molly's death has taught me anything, it's that our years on this earth aren't guaranteed. We might live to be thirteen, like Molly, or to be a hundred or to fifty-seven. Jack might die before me like Molly did. What matters is what we do with the years we have, the love we give, the life we put into each day. Who knows how Jack will grow up with us, how he'll feel, how we'll age, how long we'll be around, but I know this: he's going to be as loved as much as it's possible for a little boy to be loved. Many kids born to appropriately aged parents don't ever get that.

However, despite my fears of judgment, it turns out that most people were really inspired by my story. I've been touched by how generous and understanding friends and family and strangers have been in their response to my journey of having a baby so late in my life. For all the unkindness I've witnessed in my life, I still believe that human goodness prevails, that people care more than they hate, and that when they hate, it comes from a place of brokenness and fear.

And Brandy was hugely moved that we named our rainbow baby after the little boy she'd lost. I have a picture of her Jack on our refrigerator. I think of him and look at him every day of my life. And when Jack is old enough, I will tell him about how he got his name. That part of our job as those who get left behind, as those still living, is to remember those who have gone ahead of us. Like Jack. Like his sister, Molly.

One part of Jack's story that gives me the most hope that he will have a full, love-filled life, no matter what happens to me and to Kenny, lies with Gracie.

When we told her about being pregnant, she was devastated. Once again, my actions proved to her that she wasn't enough. But from the moment Jack was born, everything changed. She stopped looking at what I'd done, and instead, she looked into the eyes of her little brother, this tiny baby, this new life that would be part of her life after all the loss.

And I know that she'll probably be as much of a mom as a sister to him in the way that many children have several mother figures in their lives.

We've had a few mom-grandma comments already, which have made us smile. I don't feel offended, not for a second, that someone mistakes me for a grandma. We're not used to seeing mothers as old as me holding newborns.

When we took Jack to Florida for a small family vacation, someone stopped Gracie by the pool and said they couldn't believe she was in a bikini so soon after giving birth.

At Disney World, while I was sitting at an outdoor café, giving Jack a bottle, someone stopped to tell me how kind I was to give his mom a break, that grandmas are important.

Neither of us minds these comments. Jack has both of us. We love him completely. It doesn't matter what our roles are.

And Gracie, for all the struggles she had in accepting my pregnancy and all the fights we've had since Molly's death, has fallen in love again. With Jack. With life. She has a little brother. Whenever she comes home from work or college or when she's been out with her friends, she doesn't even stop to say hi to me and Kenny anymore, she just stretches out her arms and asks, "Where is he?" And then he notices her and gives the biggest smile, like he's been waiting for her all day, and she wraps him and holds him close. He's hers as much as anyone's; perhaps he's hers most of all.

There are times when I've failed Gracie. When I've been so lost in my own grief that I haven't been able to do much more than survive a day at a time. But I do believe that having Jack has been my greatest gift to her at this time of unbearable loss. Gracie can call herself a sibling again. I've given her a new life to love. It's no longer a question of her not being enough or Jack being there to fill the hole left behind by Molly. Jack isn't a replacement for Molly and he's not compensating for a lack in

Gracie. He's just himself with his big eyes and his long skinny limbs and his determination to be alive in the world with us.

No matter how strange and unusual the circumstances of his birth, or the age of his mother, Jack was quite obviously meant to be.

Chapter 38

The Story of a Happy American Family

I was foolish to think that I could control the media narrative. Newspapers and TV shows know what stories they want to tell. And they don't have much space for the nuances and complexities of individual lives.

In the days after Jack's birth, I was contacted by more media outlets than I can count, and not just in the US. The whole world was interested in this old American woman who'd given birth at age fifty-seven to a healthy baby boy.

Between feedings and naps and trying to get used to living with a newborn again, I scheduled Zoom calls and phone interviews with reporters.

They liked the grief-to-life narrative, a story of loss and hope, of overcoming the odds.

But most of all, they wanted to paint the picture of a happy, wholesome, all-American family with their miracle baby.

Of me and Kenny, holding baby Jack.

Of big sister Gracie.

Of the happy family.

We are not that family.

Having Jack was never about fixing my relationship with Kenny or Gracie or about putting our family together again after Molly's death.

As selfish as it sounds, having Jack was about me.

I needed to have a baby.

I needed to know that I could give life again.

I needed to listen to and act on those dreams.

After the loss of a child, some couples grow closer. Most fall apart. For me and Kenny, it was neither, really. Our marriage was on the rocks before Molly died and her death didn't heal that. I have still felt some love for another man. I'm still mad at Kenny for losing our money and for not standing up for me to his family and for a million other things that have caused rifts between us for years now. And he is still mad at me.

When Molly died, we pulled together because we had to, because we had no choice, not because we somehow saw the light and fell in love again.

This baby isn't a love baby. It's not a do-over for our relationship. We are still as broken as we always were.

Don't get me wrong. When I watch Kenny with Jack, I remember the things I first loved in him. He's an amazing father. I remember at the birth how he just stared and stared at Jack in his incubator, fascinated and in love. Being a dad comes as naturally to Kenny as breathing. And I love that about him. And I know that he'll be an amazing father to Jack. But we are not the happy, all-American, overcoming-the-odds family that has been presented in the media these past months.

~

As I sit in the living room of my sister-in-law's home, Jack asleep on my chest, spring turning into summer, I think about my life and about how everything has changed and how nothing has changed at all.

Jack is a miracle. But I am still myself.

I am still the broken little girl who was told to keep a big adult secret as an abused child.

I am still the addict scared to stumble again.

I am still the woman who wants to escape the life she has and find a better one.

I am still the woman who loved the wrong men.

I am still the smart, driven, ambitious woman who wants to run faster than anyone else and do great and wonderful things in the world and for the world. And the woman who feels frustrated that I never made more of my talents, who started so many things and never saw them through to the end.

And I still miss Molly every second of every day.

Chapter 39
The Memory Chair
Saturday June 19th 2021

Molly's graduation from high school takes place on Saturday the nineteenth of June 2021.

It's been five years, one month, two weeks, and five days since Molly died.

My neighbor had a lawn sign made for us with her name as part of the graduating class to go with the signs for all the other seniors around town. She told me that she was nervous about giving me the sign; she wasn't sure that I would want it or that it was the right kind of gift. People are careful around my grief, not wanting to offend or to overstep. But if there's one piece of advice I could share with anyone who is nervous about reaching out to a grieving person, it's this: whatever it is you want to do, do it; whatever it is you want to say, say it. It's silence that's the worst. It's pretending that it never happened or worse that the person who died never existed in the first place.

By giving me that lawn sign, my neighbor was helping me to keep Molly's memory alive, something I've fought to do every day since she died.

It is the silence and the forgetting and the moving on that offends, not the words and the actions and the remembering.

This has maybe been one of the most important parts of all this for me, that the bright, shining light that was my daughter should never be forgotten. It's what I come back to again and again. More than my grief and loss. More than the tragedy of her death. I want her to be remembered. For her to have a legacy. That's why I work so hard on the foundation. That's why I'm writing this book. And that's what this graduation was about. The sign in the yard. The two pages in the yearbook. And this day with the memory chair and the best friend, Keisha, had when she was thirteen talking about what Molly meant to her and how huge the hole is that she's left behind.

We put the sign on the corner of our road, a road Molly walked up every day after school. Our street runs through a busy part of town, connecting to several main roads, so it has a lot of traffic. Often, when friends and family or just people who knew Molly drive past our house, they honk as a hello, as a sign that they still remember. I hope that every one of the cars that drive down that road sees Molly's name on that sign.

Molly's dream, aged thirteen, was to be the class valedictorian. I'm convinced she would have made it. Molly was fiercely determined and smart and when she set her eyes on a goal, she worked until she got it. I bet that if she were alive right now, she'd be sitting at the kitchen table preparing her speech.

Several years before Molly died, I joined the school board. She liked to joke that in five years' time, I'd be the one handing over her high school diploma and shaking her hand. I remember us sharing one of those looks, half wondering if that would ever be possible and half knowing that with the drive and tenacity we both had, yes, it would happen. We would both be on that stage, and it would be one of the most special moments of both our lives. And we'd probably have fought about something silly in the car on the way there too. Because that was us all over, the profound, shared moments and the fights because we were a bit too alike.

I've attended over twenty-five graduations. Several as a board member but most as a teacher and a coach. As a coach, I loved sitting there in my gown and hood from BU, watching my runners, who were such an important part of my life, picking up their diplomas. They made me so proud.

My school board years are winding down. My connection to the district lessening. It feels fitting that this is the year of Molly's graduation.

The thought that this would be when Molly would be ending high school is a turning point in my grief too.

In the fall, Molly would have been leaving me. Like other mothers out there with living children, I would be packing her up to go to college or maybe she'd spend a year in the Peace Corps, that would be like Molly. And like those mothers, I'd have an empty nest. For the past five years, I've watched Molly's friends growing up, going through their milestones, living at home as part of their families. But now they're growing up and moving on, and had she lived, she would have been moving on too. So, for the first time, I feel a connection to those mothers again.

I will keep missing Molly every second of every day, but at least I won't be looking around my house thinking that this is the place where Molly should be. I won't look into the room she shared with Gracie, expecting to find her sleeping in her bed. I won't look up the stairs, expecting her to come running down with her school bag and her dance things, ready to face a new day. I won't look at our porch door anymore, expecting her to push through it every morning and come flying back in at the end of each day. Like her friends, she will have moved on from the land of childhood.

When Kenny, Gracie, and I went to Hawaii that first winter after Molly's death, it was easier than being home because it was a place she'd never been. It was the same when we went to Disney World. We hid pictures of her and small objects—pieces of jewelry, things she loved—around the theme park.

But the ache of her absence wasn't so raw because we'd never been there with her before.

There are so many places Kenny and I still don't go back to because they would be too painful without Molly. But Hawaii felt OK. And Disney World too. And maybe, I'm hoping, this next school year might feel a bit better because in the normal course of events, she would have left, grown up, and moved on. Come the fall, she wouldn't have been part of our day-to-day lives anymore.

I picture all the kids in Molly's graduating class. The kids who have been together for thirteen years. They are leaving their parents too now. It's not just me who will be sitting in an empty house without my child.

It's not the same. Those families still get to have their children alive and part of their world. Children who will come back for holidays and vacations. Who will phone and text and be there for all the milestones.

But still, this transition brings me some comfort and closure, a chance to focus on celebrating the life Molly had with us, rather than mourning her absence. It's a small shift but a shift, nonetheless. And I'll take that.

And there's something else about this year. Dr. G., the kind doctor with the white hair from the children's hospital, the one who explained to Gracie that her sister wasn't going to wake up again, told me that it would take a good five years before I started feeling anything close to myself again. His words didn't really sink in at the time. I didn't know how to get through the next five minutes; five years felt like another universe. But he was right. Something has shifted this year. The grief, though ever present, isn't as oppressive as it was at first. Some days, I feel like I can breathe again.

With Molly's class graduating comes a ton of new emotions too.

As I sit there, I know that I won't be listening to Molly giving her speech as the class valedictorian and I won't be shaking her hand as she receives her diploma. I won't get to watch her throwing her cap into the air or take her home afterward and celebrate. But there is a special part of the graduation ceremony that will be Molly's. And mine. I will introduce the Memory Chair speaker, which, this year, will be Molly's best friend, Keisha.

The Memory Chair is a powerful symbol, an empty chair placed in front of the stage. It bears a single white rose. It's a physical reminder of all the losses we've suffered in our lives. The people that are missing from our lives. The people we would love to be there on this special day, celebrating with us but for one reason or another can't be. It's a common practice at military ceremonies where living with the memory of the fallen and the absent is a way of life. In those ceremonies, a star-spangled banner is folded up and placed on the chair.

Our local high school set up the Memory Chair in 2003 in memory of two local kids, a brother and sister, Sarah and Philip Gehring, who disappeared. It took two years to find their bodies. They'd been murdered by their father.

When Sarah and Philip disappeared, it was all over the news. Their mother was frantic. Sarah and Philip's friends were terrified. None of it made sense. It's another example of how different one mother's grief is from another's. I lost Molly under terrible circumstances but nothing like what their mother, Terri, went through. And Molly's death wasn't gruesome or personal. I feel grateful that I got to say goodbye. And I feel grateful that she wasn't murdered.

The Memory Chair was put in place the year Sarah would have graduated to acknowledge that she should have been part of their graduating classes. It was a way to honor Sarah and her brother's memories as well as the lives of their friends and family who had to go through this milestone without them. It was an invitation for Terri to come watch Sarah's friends graduate.

Every year, someone from the graduating class is chosen to give the Memory Chair speech. Sometimes, they speak about a parent they've lost who should have been there to watch them graduate. Sometimes, it's more subtle than that. One year, a senior talked about the years she'd lost to mental illness and the high school experiences she would never have, another spoke of a father he never knew, and another addressed life as a refugee with the chair representing those who helped her along the way. The many faces of loss and grief the Memory Chair speeches address is a reminder to us that loss is a chimera, a beast which comes in so many forms that it's impossible to pin down and define.

The Memory Chair gives all of us permission to talk about the things we've lost. And in a world that doesn't tolerate much of that, this space is important. Every year since Molly died, the chair has given me permission to think about and talk about Molly. Like her absence from what would have been her first year at high school. Like the year that Gracie graduated and spoke about her sister being missing from her graduation. It gives someone struggling with mental illness permission to talk about their pain. It gives a child permission to talk about their parent who is absent because they're in prison or because they've been taken away from them through divorce or because they died.

We need this kind of permission. To talk. To share our stories. To be heard and seen in our loss.

I spent some time trying to plan my speech but I'm not good at that. I give speeches off-the-cuff, I'm spontaneous, I like to feel the moment and reflect the mood of the audience. I'm a bit scared that I'll let Molly down but I'm also old enough to know that this is the way I work best. I show up fully in the moment and usually that's enough.

~

Gracie sits beside me in the car as we drive the short distance between our house to Memorial Field. She's wearing an elegant, navy, short-sleeved romper. She looks so grown up. Calm and composed. Her blonde hair swept over her shoulders. Her skin already tanned from the sun. She graduated two years ago now. That year, she was the one who gave the Memory Chair speech, sharing her feelings about not having her sister with her on her graduation day. But she's already a different person now from that high school student standing on the podium. She's training to be an early childhood teacher. She has a steady boyfriend. School is a distant memory.

I'm in the pink dress I wore at her funeral with the dirty pink crocks I use to walk around the yard. Like my off-the-cuff speech, it's a more authentic version of myself than getting all dressed up. I'm wearing Molly's favorite color. And I'm wearing a dress. And my hair is down, long and blonde and curly again. It's about as dolled up as I ever get. I'm still me and me is something I'm never prepared to compromise on. I am what I am; take me or leave me.

It's a hot, blue-skied day, hardly a cloud. Gracie goes to find her chair on the field while I join the rest of the school board. I look around and see the lines of crimson gowns and hoods on either side of the track field that I've coached on for decades. Away from my house, this is as close as I get to home. The bleachers are full. Music is playing from the loudspeakers. Flags are flying. Hundreds of chairs are lined up in front of the main podium.

After over a year of being frightened to gather, of standing apart and wearing masks, this feels miraculous. Molly would have been relieved that she got to graduate in person rather than through a TV screen, a small compensation for having lost out on so many of her senior experiences because of COVID.

As the high school band and orchestra play *Pomp and Circumstance,* March no.1 by Edward Elgar, the seniors file to their seats. A few students stop to hug me. I've shared a journey with so many of those kids. In the classroom. On the track. With Molly. Kids who have been through our house and our lives and are now all grown up. They're all fizzing with excitement, their smiles wide, their steps light and full of energy. No matter how hard the past year has been or how much of a struggle it's been to graduate, today is their day.

Then we stand by our seats for "The Star-Spangled Banner" sung by the choir. I can already feel goosebumps rising on my arms. Molly would have loved every part of this day. The dressing up. The gown. Decorating her cap with all the things she loved. The singing and the music, the waiting and the walking to her chair on the field. She would have been preparing for it for days like she prepared for Christmas Day or Halloween or birthdays. I can feel her excitement here buzzing in the air.

The Memory Chair Speech comes near the beginning. I walk onto the stage and look out at the sea of faces. I wonder which chair Molly would have sat in and how she would have looked as a young woman.

I talk about Molly's friend Skylar who should have been here today but who had an epileptic seizure and is in the hospital where Molly spent a week, lying unconscious, a reminder, if we needed one, that every day there are unexpected twists to our lives. That, as Molly's death taught me and COVID has taught all of us, nothing is certain, nothing stays the same.

That is the theme of my speech. That we like to divide life into neat, linear chapters. That we want life to make sense. That we expect to go from one milestone to the next without interruption. Graduations and weddings. But the truth is that our exits from life aren't equal. Some people leave us at the very moment we expect them to be alongside us most vividly. I can't imagine a brighter, stronger, more vivid presence than thirteen-year-old Molly. She should have lived out her thirteenth year and all the ones after that that led to this day. She shouldn't have left us so early. But she did, and many others do too. Life isn't linear. The chapters don't follow in a neat narrative. Those of us who have lost people we love understand that.

I talk about the origins of the chair and how in the military we sign up for the possibility of losing someone. The Memory Chair makes sense there more than anywhere. We don't expect to lose our children as they're going about their everyday lives. Choosing a pink dress at the mall one day and falling into a coma the next.

I talk about how the chair isn't just about missing people, it's about anything that is missing from our lives on this big day.

I talk about the importance of sharing our struggles, that keeping them secret and locked away rarely helps us. I talk about how each year the Memory Chair allows us to share our painful and beautiful stories.

I talk about how significant it is that Skylar, lying in the hospital today, was Molly's first best friend, how they'd send each other crayon letters. And how Keisha, giving the speech today, was Molly's last best friend. So many beginnings and so many endings wrapped up in this day for all of us.

And I talk about how the Memory Chair isn't just there to honor the people who are missing but those who are sitting here, living their lives and feeling the absence of those they loved and lost. Gracie made that point to me once. That the chair is for those of us left behind.

If I think back to all the Memory Chair speeches I've heard, they have this in common: they seek to make meaning from the meaningless, to connect the absent to the present.

At one point, I hear a baby crying, and my whole body shifts. My eyes dart around the field, and I spot Kenny, pushing Jack in a stroller on the perimeter of the field by the bleachers. Molly's two-month-old baby brother, a baby brother who would never have existed had it not been for her death, taking in the sun and the blue sky and the sounds of his big sister's graduation.

Jack will never make up for Molly's absence, but I know that his life and her death are connected in a way that I will never fully understand but that I feel deep in my soul as a mother. And I know that today they are both here, in their way and that they feel it too.

I finish my speech and then I introduce Keisha and take my seat.

She is nothing like the little girl with frizzy hair and a big smile who came for sleepovers at my house with her sister, Rebekah. She is a young woman now. Which catches me off guard. I realize, again, that Molly would be different from how I remember her. That she would be a young woman too. The change in Keisha is even more overwhelming because I haven't really seen her these past four years. After sitting at Molly's bedside and reading a four-page letter to her as her way of saying goodbye, Keisha left the hospital with her mom, and then her grief took her to a quiet, private place. We all grieve so differently. Mine has been loud and public. I've needed people to hear me and to see me and to let me know that Molly was real and that they still remember her. Keisha managed her loss differently. But we've both made it to this point, to this day, and the young woman standing up there in her gown and cap is breathtaking.

In her speech, she honors two girls who should have been here today: Natalie and Molly. She speaks about how, alongside their too-early deaths, they shared a love for the color pink. She speaks of their characters and how much they are missed. And she makes clear how inadequate language is in capturing how hard it is to lose people we love, that the words grief and anguish and misery and sorrow do nothing but point vaguely in the direction of some much greater, wordless pain.

And then she begins to speak of the greater losses this country and the world have experienced this past year. And Keisha isn't the only student who takes her speech in this direction. The salutatorian, the valedictorian, and the class president all take up a similar thread. And it's striking. Considering that this day is about them and that they are at a stage in their lives where they might be forgiven a little self-centeredness, all three of these girls look outward. They make clear that this graduation day—and for Keisha, this Memory Chair—is not just about their one class and their one school and this moment standing on Memorial Field in our town in New Hampshire. It's about remembering the many injustices that America has faced this year: the pain and loss of being Black in America. The Asian American citizens who have faced hatred and discrimination. Echoing the poem by Amanda Gorman who read her words at Joe Biden's inauguration, Keisha speaks of the hill that they've all climbed to get to Memorial Field today and the many classmates, literal and figurative, left behind when the climb had barely started, those who never had the chance to get here.

The way in which Keisha takes the Memory Chair speech into the wider arena of race and injustice, the political awareness she shows, as do the other speakers, raises the hairs on the back of my neck. Molly would have fit right in here. She would have given a speech today and she, too, would have addressed these bigger world issues. When Molly was eleven, her fifth-grade teacher shared with me an essay she wrote about Malala. And in her short life, she stood up for every injustice she ever saw, especially the injustices on her doorstep: the kids who didn't feel at home in the cafeteria, the custodian who was invisible because his job wasn't valued, the boy whose parents couldn't afford to give him a scooter, or the friend who didn't get an Easter basket. Molly would have been enraged by all the unnecessary deaths brought on by the mishandling of the COVID epidemic. She would have been enraged by the racial injustice splitting her country apart at the seams. She would have been the first to stand up for LGBTQ+ rights. The first to protest, to write letters, to sign petitions, to speak out. By speaking of these things, Keisha honored Molly and her memory more than she'll ever know.

There was another point in the ceremony that made me

think of Molly and her character and how her spirit lived on in this class. The school board president, Jim Richards, spoke about the overwhelming capacity for kindness and compassion that marked the graduating class of 2021. That they took care of each other. High school kids are not always known for their kindness. It can be a brutal time. A survival of the fittest regime that cares little for the misfits or those left behind. But Jim Richards was right, this class was different. They picked each other up when they fell. They lived out their kindness in a thousand ways, seen and unseen. I like to think that maybe they carried a little of Molly's spirit with them.

And then it's done. Every one of those 380 students has walked across the stage and had their name read aloud and picked up their graduation certificate and heard the cheers rise around them as they turn in the morning sun to face their friends and family and smile. I work out where Molly would have been, near the beginning, being a Banzhoff. I feel a beat between one student walking off the stage and another walking on, the beat where she should have been. I like to think she would have had one of those extra loud cheers that those students get who have somehow made a special mark on their peers and teachers. Not because she was the most popular but because she touched the greatest number of lives. The cheers wouldn't have come up from a particular sports team she played on or a group of fashionable kids. The cheers would have been dotted around the whole of Memorial Field and they would have stretched far beyond too.

The last day I drove Molly to school, the week before the April vacation which would end in her death, I remember her pausing before getting out of the car.

"I know where I fit in now," she told me. "I'm not a member of any group. I have friends in all the groups. So, I belong everywhere."

I think of the janitor who came to say goodbye to Molly and the bus driver and the elementary school teacher who no longer teaches but still remembers Molly and the kid from the projects who got a scooter because Molly saved up points for him through her own achievements and good behavior and the other kid who got her Easter Basket and all those kids in middle school who didn't have to face the social humiliation of the cafeteria but could come together in that classroom and sit at a desk and open their lunch boxes and feel safe. I think of the kids who sat with her in the orchestra and who performed with her on stage and who did projects with her and the girls who danced with her at the dance academy and those who lived in and out of our house because Molly made them feel welcome and at home in a way that they sometimes didn't feel in their own families.

Yes, in my proud mother's heart, I'd like to think that Molly would have got the loudest cheer. And even though that beat between those two students is silent for most, to me, the cheers ring loud, so loud that the whole blue sky is alive with the voices of those who knew and loved her.

When all the seniors, now graduated, are back at their seats, there are some closing comments, and then they all stand and throw their caps high up in the air, a sea of crimson against the blue sky and the hot sun. For a second, they're no longer individuals, no longer separate names and kids with separate lives heading in separate directions. They're all one, their caps suspended in the air, their hands outstretched, and Molly is as much there as any of them standing there in their gowns.

And then the caps drop back to the ground.

And the present clicks back in.

As the music starts and it's time for everyone to leave, it hits me, like it's hit me a million times before when I've somehow been swept up into how things should be and forgotten how they really are: she won't be coming home with us.

I watch the graduates file out of their seats, messily this time, not like the neat procession at the beginning of the ceremony. They're done with the ritual. They're giddy from the joy and freedom of having made it, of having got through high school. And they look across Memorial Field to their parents and their siblings and their grandparents and their extended family waiting with smiles and flowers and balloons.

As the field empties, Gracie and I go over to the Memory Chair. We place some flowers on the chair and take some pictures. We think of Molly who was so much with us today and so achingly absent.

And then we walk back to the car and drive home.

Chapter 40

The Brown Couch

After Molly's graduation, I realize that it's time to start letting some things go, just like if she were still alive, I'd be letting her go from our home and out into the world.

Molly would have graduated along with her class of 2021. She'd be an adult, she sure as hell would be letting me *know* she was an adult, and she'd be moving on from her childhood home and her childhood things. So, perhaps, I tell myself, it's time for me to move on too, to reclaim this house and everything in it for the future.

Just as the moms of living children who graduated this year are spending the summer taking down the posters in their kids' rooms and packing up boxes of books and clothes, filling their cars with memories that will travel with their children into the next stage of their lives, it's time for me to move into the next stage of my life too. I need to pack some boxes and take down some posters.

For a long time, the thought of getting rid of anything in the house that held memories of Molly was unbearable to me. Even those things bound up in the unhappy memories had to stay because any removal felt like a loss, a getting rid of Molly herself, limb by limb.

Since her death, I've seen it as a personal mission to keep Molly and everything about who and how she was in the world alive. The objects themselves don't matter. The house doesn't matter. But the fact that Molly touched them and lived in and with them, that matters. That's why I haven't let anything be tossed out.

But my grief is beginning to shift. And with it my relationship to all those things I haven't been able to let go of.

I'm coming to realize that it's time to put my memories of Molly somewhere else, somewhere better. That these things I associated with Molly are no longer serving me and my grief.

When Molly was still alive, everything about our house was an expression of our family and how we lived and loved. It was never one of those neat, clean, showroom houses. Every inch of it was lived in.

When Molly died, the house became a place where we just existed. No one truly lived here anymore, not in the way we had with Molly. We moved from room to room in a daze. No new memories were formed.

It's been seven years now. I know that things must change. That if I'm going to move forward and make something meaningful of the next twenty-five years of my life, I must do it now.

The process started last summer when Gracie reclaimed her bedroom, the one she'd shared with Molly. For four years, that room remained untouched. The bed was the same as it was the morning Molly ran to the bathroom to be sick. Her phone plugged into the wall socket. The things she'd bought at Rockingham Mall—candles and bath salts and candy—still on her desk. We were scared that if we moved even one thing, we would lose her altogether. Any sign of her having been in our family and our home would vanish. But for Gracie, it was time.

As I watched her sifting through and moving Molly's things, boxing things up, changing the furniture around, turning it from the room of two young teenage girls into the room of a young woman, I felt like parts of my body were being torn off. But now when I walk past that room, I feel calm. There's no longer that tightening in my chest when I'd look at Molly's twin bed expecting her to still be in it. It was right to move on. Just like it's right to move on with the couch too.

A friend with a truck helps Kenny get it out of the house. He's English. He has a sense of humor but he's kind too. When he sees my eyes tear up over the couch, he understands.

I tell him about how my parents bought that couch in the eighties for their new house in Webster. I remember thinking how fancy it was. They gave it to me in 1997 when I moved into my first home. It was my first real piece of furniture as an adult, and I haven't had another couch since.

My water broke on that couch when I was pregnant with Gracie. We'd been living in our house almost a year. When Gracie was a baby, I'd come home from a long day of teaching or coaching track to find my mother on that coach, Gracie fast asleep on her chest.

And then, as that room began to fill with toys, especially when Molly came along too, that couch was always the background. I have a thousand pictures of that room and the couch is always there, standing in the background, propping up our lives.

I remember breastfeeding Molly on that couch. She was teeny-tiny, maybe three-to-four weeks old. She couldn't look at me properly yet, her eyes weren't able to focus, but for a second, I felt her eyes lock with mine. My neck hairs went up. In those big, wise eyes of hers, I felt like she was an old soul and letting me know the full extent of who she was and who she was going to be. *I know I'm human and I'm here,* that look said. It was my first real spiritual experience with Molly. Then suddenly she went back to having her baby shark eyes, and I went back to nursing.

One day, when I came home from track practice, Molly, not quite two, toddled over. She sat in my lap and lifted my shirt and said, "Here you are 'bedoot,' I missed you today." She'd missed my boobs for nursing. She was both hilarious and heartbreaking in that way that two-year-olds do so well.

As the years passed and the girls grew, I'd still find my mom in that room with the girls after my days at school. It would be filled with stuff. Their toys. Their craft activities. At Christmas, we'd take pictures of each other sitting on that couch in our holiday sweaters. I have a hundred photos of that room and always in the background, the brown couch. So much of raising Gracie and Molly is on the couch.

In the last year of Molly's life, we worked on tidying up the house. It was clean. They sifted through their old toys and gave them away. The girls had sleepovers with their friends sprawled between the couch and the rug. There are pictures of my sophisticated teenage girls standing by the Christmas tree after the dance show. Pictures of Molly lying on the couch, reading a book. Selfies of me and Molly or Molly and Gracie goofing. The hundreds of movies we watched together, curled up on that couch. The time a good friend disappointed me, and I felt so sad and sat on that couch crying and this time it was my girls who comforted me. The Mother's Day when I sat on the couch next to the bay window, and they fed me food and Molly played her violin.

We were growing up as a family, but we were still very much together and so many of our interactions still happened on that couch, and that room was the center of our universe. If we weren't in the kitchen or dining room eating, this room is where we lived, in this room on this couch.

I guess that's why, for a long time, I panicked about getting rid of the couch in case the memories went with it. Now I feel like I need to store the memories better. That I need to untether them from the house and the couch and Molly and Gracie's bedroom. Because with the happy memories comes the pain of absence too. Every time I look at that couch, I'm reminded of the fact that Molly's no longer here to sit on it. And I'm reminded, too, of something Kenny told me. On that Sunday morning, a few hours before she died, she lay on that couch, a blanket over her, her eyes closed, waiting for the paramedics to arrive. And I wasn't there to sit next to her or stroke her hair or to tell her that it was going to be OK.

I can't re-create the last twenty-five years to be like the next. They must be different. I'm tired of living in a house that stopped existing on May 7. It stopped existing and became a place where people just stay, not live. A place of memories and ghosts. It's time for change.

Soon, other things will go too. The rug. Other bits of furniture. I can't predict what will go when but I've started the process and the moving forward feels good.

After he's listened to all my stories, my English friend who'd come to help, sits down on the couch next to me. We can both hear the springs give way under the weight of his body, how there's no give anymore.

"Seriously, Barb," he says, his smile full of light and kindness. "This couch has got to go."

Slowly, I nod and wipe my eyes and laugh a little.

"Yeah, I know. You can take it now."

And I watch him load it out of our living room with Kenny. I watch them lift it onto the bed of the truck and then I watch them both as they back out of the driveway. I stand on the porch, listening to the truck as it disappears down the road on its way to the dump. And then I come back inside and stare at the empty room.

Afterword

Who Can Say?

There's a song that accompanies the slideshow of Molly pictures that my friend John made for the memorial. It's the closing number from the musical *Wicked*. The song is called "For Good," and it's about how our lives are changed forever by the people we meet.

Throughout the song, there's a question mark as to whether Glinda, the Good Witch of the North has been changed for the better by her best friend, Elphie, the Wicked Witch of the West.

Glinda asks whether she's been changed for the better.

I like that. The ambiguity. The honesty of that feeling.

There's an assumption that when hard things happen to us, we're meant to come out of them stronger and better and more enlightened. But the truth is, we might not. Or we might not for a very long time. And even if we do, we might slide back again and become worse, worse even than before that thing happened. Or that "better" might be tainted by something else in our life that isn't so good. Because life is messy and complicated and sometimes it just hits us so hard that we feel like we can't get up again and like nothing good could possibly come of it all. And that's OK. Having something horrible happen to us doesn't mean we have to become saints.

Some people are like that. Some people rise from the ashes

like a phoenix. The tragedy saints. But most of us are just human. For most of us, becoming better because something bad has happened isn't even an option. Just getting through the day is hard enough.

In musicals, it's different.

In the song from *Wicked*, the lyrics do change.

After the beautiful ambiguity of the first verses, the refrain switches from a question mark to the positive assertion. After everything she's been through, she believes that she has, indeed, been changed for the better.

The message is clear, positive, optimistic, linear: at some point, all the hardship will turn good and we will come out of it all better and stronger.

I get it. Musicals need happy endings.

We need happy endings.

As human beings, we crave hope. I crave hope too.

And maybe, just maybe, Glinda has it right, that if we survive, if we make it through, we are changed for the better.

But the truth is, I don't know.

And my suspicion is that even if Glinda is right, that we're changed for the better, it's more complicated than that too.

When I look back at all the things that have happened in my life from a childhood of secrecy about abuse to subsequent abusive relationships with older men, my lifetime of addiction, the bad decisions I've made along the way, and, ultimately, my loss of Molly, I'd like to think that I've been changed for the better. I *try* to think that way. To *be* that way. I've certainly learned a great deal about myself and about the world because of everything I've been through. And for Molly, to honor her memory and her goodness, I try to do better. To be better.

But the words from the song that come back to me most are these: *Who can say?*

In other words, the beginning of the song feels more honest than the end.

Because the truth of life, with all its pain and tragedy and hardship and messiness and beauty and friendship and be-trayal and love and loss, is that we don't really know, we can't really say. We can just share our stories and stay open-minded and open-hearted and always keep learning and hope—sure, always hope—but also recognize that no one truly has the an-swers. It's a beautiful kind of paradox: searching for answers is at the heart of what it means to be human, but that the only true answer we get from the universe, in my experience anyway, is that everything is a mystery. That neither the good bits nor the bad bits, the miracles or the tragedies, make much sense in the end. Or not from this side of death, anyway. May-be Molly was right when she envied Papa Gordy for passing away because now he had all the answers.

So, we just must get on with the living. And accept that sometimes we'll do something beautiful and miraculous, like having a baby at fifty-seven, and sometimes we'll get into our cars and drive to a tree in the middle of nowhere and scream our lungs out and that both those things are in us—*are* us—and that's OK. Because that's who we are. Miserable and miraculous and broken and beautiful. And a mystery, always a mystery.

I don't know what tomorrow will hold for me, for Kenny and Gracie and baby Jack. I'm not sure where Molly is right now or what she's doing. I don't know whether any of us could have prevented her death or what the purpose of her death was. I don't know how many more years I must live or how I should live them. And I don't know whether I've been changed for good by any of this. But I do know that I'll keep showing up in every way I know how and that I'll keep embracing the mystery, which I suspect is the hardest and most beautiful thing any of us can do.

Acknowledgments

If it takes a thousand tiny steps to get through child loss back to some kind of hope, it also takes a thousand tiny steps to make a book, to tell the story of what happened. While I owe the greatest of thanks to the novelist Virginia Macgregor, my ghostwriter, for being willing to put her pen to Molly's story and bring it to life, there are several heroes who have contributed to the story itself.

The whole team at Atmosphere Press, who have worked with such professionalism and passion to bring Motherland to the world.

Debra Stanley for her brilliant proof-reading skills and for supporting me through my grief.

My local arts community and Cindy Flanagan's dance academy, RB Production's Clint Klose, PEG and CTP Director Karen Braz, and CCANH's Steve Martin. All not only created her beautiful memorial show, *MollyB the Musical*, but maintain their role as her biggest supporters, as through the MollyB Foundation, we try to bring the joy of dance and theater to any child who wants it.

The Tuesday Night Girls, Kelsey, Rachel, Chloe, Emmalena, Maegan, Shelby, and Meaghan who gave Gracie hope on that awful night.

Miss Hillary and Mr. Bourasa who remember Molly daily and provide continued love and support to Gracie and me in our grief.

The hundreds of friends who came to see Molly those last days of her life and those few who continue to show up for us.

Especially Polly for unwavering understanding and authenticity and Deb for sitting with me and holding my legs in her lap when all I can do is breathe.

The Hunger family, for returning our embrace and then sharing their Rachel with us.

Robyn, for always being at my side during that week when Molly was in hospital, and in the year that followed.

Karen Kenny for helping me learn to forgive myself, which was a big part of my therapy around grief.

Margaret Porter for reading an early draft of the book and offering helpful comments.

All of those in the medical world who helped Molly and then helped me in the treatment of my tumors and the creation and birth of Jack, most notably Dr. Chaudhari, Dr. Eskandar, and Dr. Cardone.

My family, both nuclear and extended, for stepping up again and again to honor Kenny, Gracie, and me in our grief.

The many grief communities and the grieving individuals who have given me comfort, who have seen me and heard me and helped me feel less alone. Most of all, I'd like to thank Brandy, the mother of a little boy who died, called Jack, who gave me the honor of naming my Jack after hers and for being such a support in all my crazy, crazy moments in grief. 'I would also like to thank Lisa, Cathy, and Big Ed, the parents of Marilee, Vinnie and Molly, children who died far too young and who have visited me in my dreams, for creating such love and support in the face of child loss.

You are my island.

Kenny, for getting up every day and keeping the flow of the household going.

Gracie, for not only surviving the most horrible of losses but growing and developing into an amazing ambassador of love and light, for taking all of life's lessons and using them to become better and stronger, for not giving up. And for being the best big sister in the world to Jack.

And, of course, I want to thank my two children who book-end this memoir.

Molly, for the miracle that her life was and the amazing legacy that she's left behind. Thank you for giving me the honor of being your mother, even if it was for a painfully brief time. I know that wherever you are, you are still working to make the world a better place, that you are touching and changing lives.

And finally, thank you sweet, delicious Jack Jack, for (against oh so many odds) making me a mother again. For bringing me back to life. For giving me hope and joy and faith that it is possible to live after the worst that has happened. You are the light of our lives.

Where to Find Help

Not long after I lost Molly, I joined a few online grief groups, where, unlike in my immediate, day to day life, I found people who understood what I was going through, and that was a huge balm. Everyone's grief is different, of course, but there are similarities in the landscape that, when shared, can help you feel less alone.

In the hurry and bustle and speed and sheer aliveness of everyday life, it sometimes feels like there isn't much space in the world for those of us who are grieving. These grief groups became my island: a place where I felt seen and at home. Below are some of the ones I joined. There are many others out there. Try some out, until you find your own island.

I also found great comfort from books. At times, grief is so physically and mentally debilitating, that it feels impossible to read. But there will come a time when the right book, the right voice, will speak to you. Below are some that helped me.

I've also included links to my own podcast, newsletter and social media, where I speak regularly, and with the same openness and honesty as in this book. I hope I can be there for you. Please reach out if you need to talk.

Books

Languages of Loss: A psychotherapist's journey through grief by Sasha Bates

The Year of Magical Thinking by Joan Didion

Once More We Saw Stars by Jayson Greene

Comfort by Ann Hood

On Grief and Grieving by David Kessler

Finding Meaning by David Kessler

You Are the Mother of All Mothers: A Message of Hope for the Grieving Heart by Angela Miller

Sad Book by Michael Rosen

The Archaeology of Loss: Life, love and the art of dying by Sarah Tarlow

The Shack by William P. Young

Grief Groups

Ellie's Way:
http://www.elliesway.org

Eluna: Camp Erin: Where Children and Teens Learn to Grieve and Heal
https://elunanetwork.org/camps-programs/camp-erin

The Compassionate Friends: Supporting Family After a Child Dies:
https://www.compassionatefriends.org

A Bed for My Heart:
https://abedformyheart.com

Facebook Groups

Child Loss, Our Children in the Stars

Friend of Vinnie Meiers Support Group

LINKS TO MY OWN WORK:

The MollyB Foundation

https://mollybfoundation.org

The MollyB Foundation was established to help children in need with the opportunity to find their voice and create happiness through participation in activities that support positive mental health and inclusion. Molly's mission was to make people happy and her foundation assures she can continue to do so. You can contribute by following the links on the website.

A Thousand Tiny Steps
Ordinary People. Extraordinary Circumstances

https://athousandtinysteps.com

In sharing the stories of my life, I hope to clear the path so we may all find joy in the face of tragedy and see light in the darkness.

Podcast:
https://athousandtinysteps.com/the-podcast/

Blog:
https://athousandtinysteps.com/blog/

Instagram:
https://www.instagram.com/barb_444/

Facebook:
https://www.facebook.com/barb.higgins.96

About the Author

BARB HIGGINS is mother to Gracie, Molly, Jack, and Baby Gordy. In 2016, she lost Molly to a brain tumor. In 2021, aged 57, she gave birth to her little boy, Jack. To date, she is the oldest woman to have given birth in New Hampshire.

An educator at heart, she also loves athletics, music, theater and the arts. Barb graduated from Boston University in 1986 with a Masters in Education. She also has a Certificate of Advanced Graduate Studies (C.A.G.S.) from Plymouth State University in Education Leadership through Arts Integration. She has taught elementary, special, and physical education as well as health. She has coached cross- country and track and field for over 30 years. A Division One All American in Track and Field at BU in 1983, Barb was a competitive runner for many years competing for Nike before returning to her hometown in 1989.

Barb coaches and participates in Crossfit and has a Podcast called *A Thousand Tiny Steps*. Creating The MollyB Foundation helps to keep the best parts of Molly alive and helps others to achieve their goals.

Every day, Barb shares her thoughts of what it means to live in Motherland in the hope that it will help mothers everywhere feel comforted, seen and understood.

She lives in New Hampshire with her Kenny and her two living children, Gracie and Jack.

About Atmosphere Press

Founded in 2015, Atmosphere Press was built on the principles of Honesty, Transparency, Professionalism, Kindness, and Making Your Book Awesome. As an ethical and author-friendly hybrid press, we stay true to that founding mission today.

If you're a reader, enter our giveaway for a free book here:

SCAN TO ENTER
BOOK GIVEAWAY

If you're a writer, submit your manuscript for consideration here:

SCAN TO SUBMIT
MANUSCRIPT

And always feel free to visit Atmosphere Press and our authors online at atmospherepress.com. See you there soon!